C-1234 CAREER EXAMINATION SERIES

This is your
PASSBOOK for...

Associate Management Analyst

Test Preparation Study Guide
Questions & Answers

COPYRIGHT NOTICE

This book is SOLELY intended for, is sold ONLY to, and its use is RESTRICTED to individual, bona fide applicants or candidates who qualify by virtue of having seriously filed applications for appropriate license, certificate, professional and/or promotional advancement, higher school matriculation, scholarship, or other legitimate requirements of education and/or governmental authorities.

This book is NOT intended for use, class instruction, tutoring, training, duplication, copying, reprinting, excerption, or adaptation, etc., by:

1) Other publishers
2) Proprietors and/or Instructors of "Coaching" and/or Preparatory Courses
3) Personnel and/or Training Divisions of commercial, industrial, and governmental organizations
4) Schools, colleges, or universities and/or their departments and staffs, including teachers and other personnel
5) Testing Agencies or Bureaus
6) Study groups which seek by the purchase of a single volume to copy and/or duplicate and/or adapt this material for use by the group as a whole without having purchased individual volumes for each of the members of the group
7) Et al.

Such persons would be in violation of appropriate Federal and State statutes.

PROVISION OF LICENSING AGREEMENTS – Recognized educational, commercial, industrial, and governmental institutions and organizations, and others legitimately engaged in educational pursuits, including training, testing, and measurement activities, may address request for a licensing agreement to the copyright owners, who will determine whether, and under what conditions, including fees and charges, the materials in this book may be used them. In other words, a licensing facility exists for the legitimate use of the material in this book on other than an individual basis. However, it is asseverated and affirmed here that the material in this book CANNOT be used without the receipt of the express permission of such a licensing agreement from the Publishers. Inquiries re licensing should be addressed to the company, attention rights and permissions department.

All rights reserved, including the right of reproduction in whole or in part, in any form or by any means, electronic or mechanical, including photocopying, recording, or by any information storage and retrieval system, without permission in writing from the Publisher.

Copyright © 2024 by
National Learning Corporation

212 Michael Drive, Syosset, NY 11791
(516) 921-8888 • www.passbooks.com
E-mail: info@passbooks.com

PASSBOOK® SERIES

THE *PASSBOOK® SERIES* has been created to prepare applicants and candidates for the ultimate academic battlefield – the examination room.

At some time in our lives, each and every one of us may be required to take an examination – for validation, matriculation, admission, qualification, registration, certification, or licensure.

Based on the assumption that every applicant or candidate has met the basic formal educational standards, has taken the required number of courses, and read the necessary texts, the *PASSBOOK® SERIES* furnishes the one special preparation which may assure passing with confidence, instead of failing with insecurity. Examination questions – together with answers – are furnished as the basic vehicle for study so that the mysteries of the examination and its compounding difficulties may be eliminated or diminished by a sure method.

This book is meant to help you pass your examination provided that you qualify and are serious in your objective.

The entire field is reviewed through the huge store of content information which is succinctly presented through a provocative and challenging approach – the question-and-answer method.

A climate of success is established by furnishing the correct answers at the end of each test.

You soon learn to recognize types of questions, forms of questions, and patterns of questioning. You may even begin to anticipate expected outcomes.

You perceive that many questions are repeated or adapted so that you can gain acute insights, which may enable you to score many sure points.

You learn how to confront new questions, or types of questions, and to attack them confidently and work out the correct answers.

You note objectives and emphases, and recognize pitfalls and dangers, so that you may make positive educational adjustments.

Moreover, you are kept fully informed in relation to new concepts, methods, practices, and directions in the field.

You discover that you are actually taking the examination all the time: you are preparing for the examination by "taking" an examination, not by reading extraneous and/or supererogatory textbooks.

In short, this PASSBOOK®, used directedly, should be an important factor in helping you to pass your test.

ASSOCIATE MANAGEMENT ANALYST

DUTIES:
Under general supervision, performs difficult professional work in the conduct of management surveys, evaluation of organizational structures, policies, practices, and operations of agencies; performs related work.

EXAMPLES OF TYPICAL TASKS:
Conducts management surveys and studies of the operations of agencies, involving analyses of organizational structures, operational and accounting systems, methods, procedures, systems, manpower requirements, utilization of machines and equipment, space layouts, forms design, records management, and other aspects of administrative management; prepares comprehensive reports of findings with recommendations for improved efficiency; discusses recommended proposals with agency heads and arranges for and directs the installation of accepted proposals; may supervise one or more subordinate analysts and technicians.

TESTS:
The test may include questions on project management; work measurement; cost analysis and cost accounting; organization, systems and procedures; governmental organization and functions; administrative techniques; communications; and related areas pertaining to the work of the candidate's own agency.

HOW TO TAKE A TEST

I. YOU MUST PASS AN EXAMINATION

A. WHAT EVERY CANDIDATE SHOULD KNOW

Examination applicants often ask us for help in preparing for the written test. What can I study in advance? What kinds of questions will be asked? How will the test be given? How will the papers be graded?

As an applicant for a civil service examination, you may be wondering about some of these things. Our purpose here is to suggest effective methods of advance study and to describe civil service examinations.

Your chances for success on this examination can be increased if you know how to prepare. Those "pre-examination jitters" can be reduced if you know what to expect. You can even experience an adventure in good citizenship if you know why civil service exams are given.

B. WHY ARE CIVIL SERVICE EXAMINATIONS GIVEN?

Civil service examinations are important to you in two ways. As a citizen, you want public jobs filled by employees who know how to do their work. As a job seeker, you want a fair chance to compete for that job on an equal footing with other candidates. The best-known means of accomplishing this two-fold goal is the competitive examination.

Exams are widely publicized throughout the nation. They may be administered for jobs in federal, state, city, municipal, town or village governments or agencies.

Any citizen may apply, with some limitations, such as the age or residence of applicants. Your experience and education may be reviewed to see whether you meet the requirements for the particular examination. When these requirements exist, they are reasonable and applied consistently to all applicants. Thus, a competitive examination may cause you some uneasiness now, but it is your privilege and safeguard.

C. HOW ARE CIVIL SERVICE EXAMS DEVELOPED?

Examinations are carefully written by trained technicians who are specialists in the field known as "psychological measurement," in consultation with recognized authorities in the field of work that the test will cover. These experts recommend the subject matter areas or skills to be tested; only those knowledges or skills important to your success on the job are included. The most reliable books and source materials available are used as references. Together, the experts and technicians judge the difficulty level of the questions.

Test technicians know how to phrase questions so that the problem is clearly stated. Their ethics do not permit "trick" or "catch" questions. Questions may have been tried out on sample groups, or subjected to statistical analysis, to determine their usefulness.

Written tests are often used in combination with performance tests, ratings of training and experience, and oral interviews. All of these measures combine to form the best-known means of finding the right person for the right job.

II. HOW TO PASS THE WRITTEN TEST

A. NATURE OF THE EXAMINATION

To prepare intelligently for civil service examinations, you should know how they differ from school examinations you have taken. In school you were assigned certain definite pages to read or subjects to cover. The examination questions were quite detailed and usually emphasized memory. Civil service exams, on the other hand, try to discover your present ability to perform the duties of a position, plus your potentiality to learn these duties. In other words, a civil service exam attempts to predict how successful you will be. Questions cover such a broad area that they cannot be as minute and detailed as school exam questions.

In the public service similar kinds of work, or positions, are grouped together in one "class." This process is known as *position-classification*. All the positions in a class are paid according to the salary range for that class. One class title covers all of these positions, and they are all tested by the same examination.

B. FOUR BASIC STEPS

1) Study the announcement

How, then, can you know what subjects to study? Our best answer is: "Learn as much as possible about the class of positions for which you've applied." The exam will test the knowledge, skills and abilities needed to do the work.

Your most valuable source of information about the position you want is the official exam announcement. This announcement lists the training and experience qualifications. Check these standards and apply only if you come reasonably close to meeting them.

The brief description of the position in the examination announcement offers some clues to the subjects which will be tested. Think about the job itself. Review the duties in your mind. Can you perform them, or are there some in which you are rusty? Fill in the blank spots in your preparation.

Many jurisdictions preview the written test in the exam announcement by including a section called "Knowledge and Abilities Required," "Scope of the Examination," or some similar heading. Here you will find out specifically what fields will be tested.

2) Review your own background

Once you learn in general what the position is all about, and what you need to know to do the work, ask yourself which subjects you already know fairly well and which need improvement. You may wonder whether to concentrate on improving your strong areas or on building some background in your fields of weakness. When the announcement has specified "some knowledge" or "considerable knowledge," or has used adjectives like "beginning principles of..." or "advanced ... methods," you can get a clue as to the number and difficulty of questions to be asked in any given field. More questions, and hence broader coverage, would be included for those subjects which are more important in the work. Now weigh your strengths and weaknesses against the job requirements and prepare accordingly.

3) Determine the level of the position

Another way to tell how intensively you should prepare is to understand the level of the job for which you are applying. Is it the entering level? In other words, is this the position in which beginners in a field of work are hired? Or is it an intermediate or advanced level? Sometimes this is indicated by such words as "Junior" or "Senior" in the class title. Other jurisdictions use Roman numerals to designate the level – Clerk I, Clerk II, for example. The word "Supervisor" sometimes appears in the title. If the level is not indicated by the title, check the description of duties. Will you be working under very close supervision, or will you have responsibility for independent decisions in this work?

4) Choose appropriate study materials

Now that you know the subjects to be examined and the relative amount of each subject to be covered, you can choose suitable study materials. For beginning level jobs, or even advanced ones, if you have a pronounced weakness in some aspect of your training, read a modern, standard textbook in that field. Be sure it is up to date and has general coverage. Such books are normally available at your library, and the librarian will be glad to help you locate one. For entry-level positions, questions of appropriate difficulty are chosen -- neither highly advanced questions, nor those too simple. Such questions require careful thought but not advanced training.

If the position for which you are applying is technical or advanced, you will read more advanced, specialized material. If you are already familiar with the basic principles of your field, elementary textbooks would waste your time. Concentrate on advanced textbooks and technical periodicals. Think through the concepts and review difficult problems in your field.

These are all general sources. You can get more ideas on your own initiative, following these leads. For example, training manuals and publications of the government agency which employs workers in your field can be useful, particularly for technical and professional positions. A letter or visit to the government department involved may result in more specific study suggestions, and certainly will provide you with a more definite idea of the exact nature of the position you are seeking.

III. KINDS OF TESTS

Tests are used for purposes other than measuring knowledge and ability to perform specified duties. For some positions, it is equally important to test ability to make adjustments to new situations or to profit from training. In others, basic mental abilities not dependent on information are essential. Questions which test these things may not appear as pertinent to the duties of the position as those which test for knowledge and information. Yet they are often highly important parts of a fair examination. For very general questions, it is almost impossible to help you direct your study efforts. What we can do is to point out some of the more common of these general abilities needed in public service positions and describe some typical questions.

1) General information

Broad, general information has been found useful for predicting job success in some kinds of work. This is tested in a variety of ways, from vocabulary lists to questions about current events. Basic background in some field of work, such as sociology or economics, may be sampled in a group of questions. Often these are principles which have become familiar to most persons through exposure rather than through formal training. It is difficult to advise you how to study for these questions; being alert to the world around you is our best suggestion.

2) Verbal ability

An example of an ability needed in many positions is verbal or language ability. Verbal ability is, in brief, the ability to use and understand words. Vocabulary and grammar tests are typical measures of this ability. Reading comprehension or paragraph interpretation questions are common in many kinds of civil service tests. You are given a paragraph of written material and asked to find its central meaning.

3) **Numerical ability**
   Number skills can be tested by the familiar arithmetic problem, by checking paired lists of numbers to see which are alike and which are different, or by interpreting charts and graphs. In the latter test, a graph may be printed in the test booklet which you are asked to use as the basis for answering questions.

4) **Observation**
   A popular test for law-enforcement positions is the observation test. A picture is shown to you for several minutes, then taken away. Questions about the picture test your ability to observe both details and larger elements.

5) **Following directions**
   In many positions in the public service, the employee must be able to carry out written instructions dependably and accurately. You may be given a chart with several columns, each column listing a variety of information. The questions require you to carry out directions involving the information given in the chart.

6) **Skills and aptitudes**
   Performance tests effectively measure some manual skills and aptitudes. When the skill is one in which you are trained, such as typing or shorthand, you can practice. These tests are often very much like those given in business school or high school courses. For many of the other skills and aptitudes, however, no short-time preparation can be made. Skills and abilities natural to you or that you have developed throughout your lifetime are being tested.

Many of the general questions just described provide all the data needed to answer the questions and ask you to use your reasoning ability to find the answers. Your best preparation for these tests, as well as for tests of facts and ideas, is to be at your physical and mental best. You, no doubt, have your own methods of getting into an exam-taking mood and keeping "in shape." The next section lists some ideas on this subject.

IV. KINDS OF QUESTIONS

Only rarely is the "essay" question, which you answer in narrative form, used in civil service tests. Civil service tests are usually of the short-answer type. Full instructions for answering these questions will be given to you at the examination. But in case this is your first experience with short-answer questions and separate answer sheets, here is what you need to know:

1) **Multiple-choice Questions**
   Most popular of the short-answer questions is the "multiple choice" or "best answer" question. It can be used, for example, to test for factual knowledge, ability to solve problems or judgment in meeting situations found at work.
   A multiple-choice question is normally one of three types—
   - It can begin with an incomplete statement followed by several possible endings. You are to find the one ending which *best* completes the statement, although some of the others may not be entirely wrong.
   - It can also be a complete statement in the form of a question which is answered by choosing one of the statements listed.

- It can be in the form of a problem – again you select the best answer.

Here is an example of a multiple-choice question with a discussion which should give you some clues as to the method for choosing the right answer:

When an employee has a complaint about his assignment, the action which will *best* help him overcome his difficulty is to
- A. discuss his difficulty with his coworkers
- B. take the problem to the head of the organization
- C. take the problem to the person who gave him the assignment
- D. say nothing to anyone about his complaint

In answering this question, you should study each of the choices to find which is best. Consider choice "A" – Certainly an employee may discuss his complaint with fellow employees, but no change or improvement can result, and the complaint remains unresolved. Choice "B" is a poor choice since the head of the organization probably does not know what assignment you have been given, and taking your problem to him is known as "going over the head" of the supervisor. The supervisor, or person who made the assignment, is the person who can clarify it or correct any injustice. Choice "C" is, therefore, correct. To say nothing, as in choice "D," is unwise. Supervisors have and interest in knowing the problems employees are facing, and the employee is seeking a solution to his problem.

2) True/False Questions

The "true/false" or "right/wrong" form of question is sometimes used. Here a complete statement is given. Your job is to decide whether the statement is right or wrong.

SAMPLE: A roaming cell-phone call to a nearby city costs less than a non-roaming call to a distant city.

This statement is wrong, or false, since roaming calls are more expensive.

This is not a complete list of all possible question forms, although most of the others are variations of these common types. You will always get complete directions for answering questions. Be sure you understand *how* to mark your answers – ask questions until you do.

V. RECORDING YOUR ANSWERS

Computer terminals are used more and more today for many different kinds of exams.

For an examination with very few applicants, you may be told to record your answers in the test booklet itself. Separate answer sheets are much more common. If this separate answer sheet is to be scored by machine – and this is often the case – it is highly important that you mark your answers correctly in order to get credit.

An electronic scoring machine is often used in civil service offices because of the speed with which papers can be scored. Machine-scored answer sheets must be marked with a pencil, which will be given to you. This pencil has a high graphite content which responds to the electronic scoring machine. As a matter of fact, stray dots may register as answers, so do not let your pencil rest on the answer sheet while you are pondering the correct answer. Also, if your pencil lead breaks or is otherwise defective, ask for another.

Since the answer sheet will be dropped in a slot in the scoring machine, be careful not to bend the corners or get the paper crumpled.

The answer sheet normally has five vertical columns of numbers, with 30 numbers to a column. These numbers correspond to the question numbers in your test booklet. After each number, going across the page are four or five pairs of dotted lines. These short dotted lines have small letters or numbers above them. The first two pairs may also have a "T" or "F" above the letters. This indicates that the first two pairs only are to be used if the questions are of the true-false type. If the questions are multiple choice, disregard the "T" and "F" and pay attention only to the small letters or numbers.

Answer your questions in the manner of the sample that follows:

32. The largest city in the United States is
    A. Washington, D.C.
    B. New York City
    C. Chicago
    D. Detroit
    E. San Francisco

1) Choose the answer you think is best. (New York City is the largest, so "B" is correct.)
2) Find the row of dotted lines numbered the same as the question you are answering. (Find row number 32)
3) Find the pair of dotted lines corresponding to the answer. (Find the pair of lines under the mark "B.")
4) Make a solid black mark between the dotted lines.

VI. BEFORE THE TEST

Common sense will help you find procedures to follow to get ready for an examination. Too many of us, however, overlook these sensible measures. Indeed, nervousness and fatigue have been found to be the most serious reasons why applicants fail to do their best on civil service tests. Here is a list of reminders:

- Begin your preparation early – Don't wait until the last minute to go scurrying around for books and materials or to find out what the position is all about.
- Prepare continuously – An hour a night for a week is better than an all-night cram session. This has been definitely established. What is more, a night a week for a month will return better dividends than crowding your study into a shorter period of time.
- Locate the place of the exam – You have been sent a notice telling you when and where to report for the examination. If the location is in a different town or otherwise unfamiliar to you, it would be well to inquire the best route and learn something about the building.
- Relax the night before the test – Allow your mind to rest. Do not study at all that night. Plan some mild recreation or diversion; then go to bed early and get a good night's sleep.
- Get up early enough to make a leisurely trip to the place for the test – This way unforeseen events, traffic snarls, unfamiliar buildings, etc. will not upset you.
- Dress comfortably – A written test is not a fashion show. You will be known by number and not by name, so wear something comfortable.

- Leave excess paraphernalia at home – Shopping bags and odd bundles will get in your way. You need bring only the items mentioned in the official notice you received; usually everything you need is provided. Do not bring reference books to the exam. They will only confuse those last minutes and be taken away from you when in the test room.
- Arrive somewhat ahead of time – If because of transportation schedules you must get there very early, bring a newspaper or magazine to take your mind off yourself while waiting.
- Locate the examination room – When you have found the proper room, you will be directed to the seat or part of the room where you will sit. Sometimes you are given a sheet of instructions to read while you are waiting. Do not fill out any forms until you are told to do so; just read them and be prepared.
- Relax and prepare to listen to the instructions
- If you have any physical problem that may keep you from doing your best, be sure to tell the test administrator. If you are sick or in poor health, you really cannot do your best on the exam. You can come back and take the test some other time.

VII. AT THE TEST

The day of the test is here and you have the test booklet in your hand. The temptation to get going is very strong. Caution! There is more to success than knowing the right answers. You must know how to identify your papers and understand variations in the type of short-answer question used in this particular examination. Follow these suggestions for maximum results from your efforts:

1) Cooperate with the monitor

The test administrator has a duty to create a situation in which you can be as much at ease as possible. He will give instructions, tell you when to begin, check to see that you are marking your answer sheet correctly, and so on. He is not there to guard you, although he will see that your competitors do not take unfair advantage. He wants to help you do your best.

2) Listen to all instructions

Don't jump the gun! Wait until you understand all directions. In most civil service tests you get more time than you need to answer the questions. So don't be in a hurry. Read each word of instructions until you clearly understand the meaning. Study the examples, listen to all announcements and follow directions. Ask questions if you do not understand what to do.

3) Identify your papers

Civil service exams are usually identified by number only. You will be assigned a number; you must not put your name on your test papers. Be sure to copy your number correctly. Since more than one exam may be given, copy your exact examination title.

4) Plan your time

Unless you are told that a test is a "speed" or "rate of work" test, speed itself is usually not important. Time enough to answer all the questions will be provided, but this does not mean that you have all day. An overall time limit has been set. Divide the total time (in minutes) by the number of questions to determine the approximate time you have for each question.

5) Do not linger over difficult questions

If you come across a difficult question, mark it with a paper clip (useful to have along) and come back to it when you have been through the booklet. One caution if you do this – be sure to skip a number on your answer sheet as well. Check often to be sure that you have not lost your place and that you are marking in the row numbered the same as the question you are answering.

6) Read the questions

Be sure you know what the question asks! Many capable people are unsuccessful because they failed to *read* the questions correctly.

7) Answer all questions

Unless you have been instructed that a penalty will be deducted for incorrect answers, it is better to guess than to omit a question.

8) Speed tests

It is often better NOT to guess on speed tests. It has been found that on timed tests people are tempted to spend the last few seconds before time is called in marking answers at random – without even reading them – in the hope of picking up a few extra points. To discourage this practice, the instructions may warn you that your score will be "corrected" for guessing. That is, a penalty will be applied. The incorrect answers will be deducted from the correct ones, or some other penalty formula will be used.

9) Review your answers

If you finish before time is called, go back to the questions you guessed or omitted to give them further thought. Review other answers if you have time.

10) Return your test materials

If you are ready to leave before others have finished or time is called, take ALL your materials to the monitor and leave quietly. Never take any test material with you. The monitor can discover whose papers are not complete, and taking a test booklet may be grounds for disqualification.

VIII. EXAMINATION TECHNIQUES

1) Read the general instructions carefully. These are usually printed on the first page of the exam booklet. As a rule, these instructions refer to the timing of the examination; the fact that you should not start work until the signal and must stop work at a signal, etc. If there are any *special* instructions, such as a choice of questions to be answered, make sure that you note this instruction carefully.

2) When you are ready to start work on the examination, that is as soon as the signal has been given, read the instructions to each question booklet, underline any key words or phrases, such as *least, best, outline, describe* and the like. In this way you will tend to answer as requested rather than discover on reviewing your paper that you *listed without describing*, that you selected the *worst* choice rather than the *best* choice, etc.

3) If the examination is of the objective or multiple-choice type – that is, each question will also give a series of possible answers: A, B, C or D, and you are called upon to select the best answer and write the letter next to that answer on your answer paper – it is advisable to start answering each question in turn. There may be anywhere from 50 to 100 such questions in the three or four hours allotted and you can see how much time would be taken if you read through all the questions before beginning to answer any. Furthermore, if you come across a question or group of questions which you know would be difficult to answer, it would undoubtedly affect your handling of all the other questions.

4) If the examination is of the essay type and contains but a few questions, it is a moot point as to whether you should read all the questions before starting to answer any one. Of course, if you are given a choice – say five out of seven and the like – then it is essential to read all the questions so you can eliminate the two that are most difficult. If, however, you are asked to answer all the questions, there may be danger in trying to answer the easiest one first because you may find that you will spend too much time on it. The best technique is to answer the first question, then proceed to the second, etc.

5) Time your answers. Before the exam begins, write down the time it started, then add the time allowed for the examination and write down the time it must be completed, then divide the time available somewhat as follows:
    - If 3-1/2 hours are allowed, that would be 210 minutes. If you have 80 objective-type questions, that would be an average of 2-1/2 minutes per question. Allow yourself no more than 2 minutes per question, or a total of 160 minutes, which will permit about 50 minutes to review.
    - If for the time allotment of 210 minutes there are 7 essay questions to answer, that would average about 30 minutes a question. Give yourself only 25 minutes per question so that you have about 35 minutes to review.

6) The most important instruction is to *read each question* and make sure you know what is wanted. The second most important instruction is to *time yourself properly* so that you answer every question. The third most important instruction is to *answer every question*. Guess if you have to but include something for each question. Remember that you will receive no credit for a blank and will probably receive some credit if you write something in answer to an essay question. If you guess a letter – say "B" for a multiple-choice question – you may have guessed right. If you leave a blank as an answer to a multiple-choice question, the examiners may respect your feelings but it will not add a point to your score. Some exams may penalize you for wrong answers, so in such cases *only*, you may not want to guess unless you have some basis for your answer.

7) Suggestions
    a. Objective-type questions
        1. Examine the question booklet for proper sequence of pages and questions
        2. Read all instructions carefully
        3. Skip any question which seems too difficult; return to it after all other questions have been answered
        4. Apportion your time properly; do not spend too much time on any single question or group of questions

5. Note and underline key words – *all, most, fewest, least, best, worst, same, opposite,* etc.
6. Pay particular attention to negatives
7. Note unusual option, e.g., unduly long, short, complex, different or similar in content to the body of the question
8. Observe the use of "hedging" words – *probably, may, most likely,* etc.
9. Make sure that your answer is put next to the same number as the question
10. Do not second-guess unless you have good reason to believe the second answer is definitely more correct
11. Cross out original answer if you decide another answer is more accurate; do not erase until you are ready to hand your paper in
12. Answer all questions; guess unless instructed otherwise
13. Leave time for review

b. Essay questions
   1. Read each question carefully
   2. Determine exactly what is wanted. Underline key words or phrases.
   3. Decide on outline or paragraph answer
   4. Include many different points and elements unless asked to develop any one or two points or elements
   5. Show impartiality by giving pros and cons unless directed to select one side only
   6. Make and write down any assumptions you find necessary to answer the questions
   7. Watch your English, grammar, punctuation and choice of words
   8. Time your answers; don't crowd material

8) Answering the essay question

Most essay questions can be answered by framing the specific response around several key words or ideas. Here are a few such key words or ideas:

M's: manpower, materials, methods, money, management
P's: purpose, program, policy, plan, procedure, practice, problems, pitfalls, personnel, public relations

   a. Six basic steps in handling problems:
      1. Preliminary plan and background development
      2. Collect information, data and facts
      3. Analyze and interpret information, data and facts
      4. Analyze and develop solutions as well as make recommendations
      5. Prepare report and sell recommendations
      6. Install recommendations and follow up effectiveness

   b. Pitfalls to avoid
      1. *Taking things for granted* – A statement of the situation does not necessarily imply that each of the elements is necessarily true; for example, a complaint may be invalid and biased so that all that can be taken for granted is that a complaint has been registered

2. *Considering only one side of a situation* – Wherever possible, indicate several alternatives and then point out the reasons you selected the best one
3. *Failing to indicate follow up* – Whenever your answer indicates action on your part, make certain that you will take proper follow-up action to see how successful your recommendations, procedures or actions turn out to be
4. *Taking too long in answering any single question* – Remember to time your answers properly

IX. AFTER THE TEST

Scoring procedures differ in detail among civil service jurisdictions although the general principles are the same. Whether the papers are hand-scored or graded by machine we have described, they are nearly always graded by number. That is, the person who marks the paper knows only the number – never the name – of the applicant. Not until all the papers have been graded will they be matched with names. If other tests, such as training and experience or oral interview ratings have been given, scores will be combined. Different parts of the examination usually have different weights. For example, the written test might count 60 percent of the final grade, and a rating of training and experience 40 percent. In many jurisdictions, veterans will have a certain number of points added to their grades.

After the final grade has been determined, the names are placed in grade order and an eligible list is established. There are various methods for resolving ties between those who get the same final grade – probably the most common is to place first the name of the person whose application was received first. Job offers are made from the eligible list in the order the names appear on it. You will be notified of your grade and your rank as soon as all these computations have been made. This will be done as rapidly as possible.

People who are found to meet the requirements in the announcement are called "eligibles." Their names are put on a list of eligible candidates. An eligible's chances of getting a job depend on how high he stands on this list and how fast agencies are filling jobs from the list.

When a job is to be filled from a list of eligibles, the agency asks for the names of people on the list of eligibles for that job. When the civil service commission receives this request, it sends to the agency the names of the three people highest on this list. Or, if the job to be filled has specialized requirements, the office sends the agency the names of the top three persons who meet these requirements from the general list.

The appointing officer makes a choice from among the three people whose names were sent to him. If the selected person accepts the appointment, the names of the others are put back on the list to be considered for future openings.

That is the rule in hiring from all kinds of eligible lists, whether they are for typist, carpenter, chemist, or something else. For every vacancy, the appointing officer has his choice of any one of the top three eligibles on the list. This explains why the person whose name is on top of the list sometimes does not get an appointment when some of the persons lower on the list do. If the appointing officer chooses the second or third eligible, the No. 1 eligible does not get a job at once, but stays on the list until he is appointed or the list is terminated.

X. HOW TO PASS THE INTERVIEW TEST

The examination for which you applied requires an oral interview test. You have already taken the written test and you are now being called for the interview test – the final part of the formal examination.

You may think that it is not possible to prepare for an interview test and that there are no procedures to follow during an interview. Our purpose is to point out some things you can do in advance that will help you and some good rules to follow and pitfalls to avoid while you are being interviewed.

What is an interview supposed to test?

The written examination is designed to test the technical knowledge and competence of the candidate; the oral is designed to evaluate intangible qualities, not readily measured otherwise, and to establish a list showing the relative fitness of each candidate – as measured against his competitors – for the position sought. Scoring is not on the basis of "right" and "wrong," but on a sliding scale of values ranging from "not passable" to "outstanding." As a matter of fact, it is possible to achieve a relatively low score without a single "incorrect" answer because of evident weakness in the qualities being measured.

Occasionally, an examination may consist entirely of an oral test – either an individual or a group oral. In such cases, information is sought concerning the technical knowledges and abilities of the candidate, since there has been no written examination for this purpose. More commonly, however, an oral test is used to supplement a written examination.

Who conducts interviews?

The composition of oral boards varies among different jurisdictions. In nearly all, a representative of the personnel department serves as chairman. One of the members of the board may be a representative of the department in which the candidate would work. In some cases, "outside experts" are used, and, frequently, a businessman or some other representative of the general public is asked to serve. Labor and management or other special groups may be represented. The aim is to secure the services of experts in the appropriate field.

However the board is composed, it is a good idea (and not at all improper or unethical) to ascertain in advance of the interview who the members are and what groups they represent. When you are introduced to them, you will have some idea of their backgrounds and interests, and at least you will not stutter and stammer over their names.

What should be done before the interview?

While knowledge about the board members is useful and takes some of the surprise element out of the interview, there is other preparation which is more substantive. It *is* possible to prepare for an oral interview – in several ways:

1) Keep a copy of your application and review it carefully before the interview

This may be the only document before the oral board, and the starting point of the interview. Know what education and experience you have listed there, and the sequence and dates of all of it. Sometimes the board will ask you to review the highlights of your experience for them; you should not have to hem and haw doing it.

2) Study the class specification and the examination announcement

Usually, the oral board has one or both of these to guide them. The qualities, characteristics or knowledges required by the position sought are stated in these documents. They offer valuable clues as to the nature of the oral interview. For example, if the job involves supervisory responsibilities, the announcement will usually indicate that knowledge of modern supervisory methods and the qualifications of the candidate as a supervisor will be tested. If so, you can expect such questions, frequently in the form of a hypothetical situation which you are expected to solve. NEVER go into an oral without knowledge of the duties and responsibilities of the job you seek.

3) Think through each qualification required

Try to visualize the kind of questions you would ask if you were a board member. How well could you answer them? Try especially to appraise your own knowledge and background in each area, *measured against the job sought*, and identify any areas in which you are weak. Be critical and realistic – do not flatter yourself.

4) Do some general reading in areas in which you feel you may be weak

For example, if the job involves supervision and your past experience has NOT, some general reading in supervisory methods and practices, particularly in the field of human relations, might be useful. Do NOT study agency procedures or detailed manuals. The oral board will be testing your understanding and capacity, not your memory.

5) Get a good night's sleep and watch your general health and mental attitude

You will want a clear head at the interview. Take care of a cold or any other minor ailment, and of course, no hangovers.

What should be done on the day of the interview?

Now comes the day of the interview itself. Give yourself plenty of time to get there. Plan to arrive somewhat ahead of the scheduled time, particularly if your appointment is in the fore part of the day. If a previous candidate fails to appear, the board might be ready for you a bit early. By early afternoon an oral board is almost invariably behind schedule if there are many candidates, and you may have to wait. Take along a book or magazine to read, or your application to review, but leave any extraneous material in the waiting room when you go in for your interview. In any event, relax and compose yourself.

The matter of dress is important. The board is forming impressions about you – from your experience, your manners, your attitude, and your appearance. Give your personal appearance careful attention. Dress your best, but not your flashiest. Choose conservative, appropriate clothing, and be sure it is immaculate. This is a business interview, and your appearance should indicate that you regard it as such. Besides, being well groomed and properly dressed will help boost your confidence.

Sooner or later, someone will call your name and escort you into the interview room. *This is it.* From here on you are on your own. It is too late for any more preparation. But remember, you asked for this opportunity to prove your fitness, and you are here because your request was granted.

What happens when you go in?

The usual sequence of events will be as follows: The clerk (who is often the board stenographer) will introduce you to the chairman of the oral board, who will introduce you to the other members of the board. Acknowledge the introductions before you sit down. Do not be surprised if you find a microphone facing you or a stenotypist sitting by. Oral interviews are usually recorded in the event of an appeal or other review.

Usually the chairman of the board will open the interview by reviewing the highlights of your education and work experience from your application – primarily for the benefit of the other members of the board, as well as to get the material into the record. Do not interrupt or comment unless there is an error or significant misinterpretation; if that is the case, do not hesitate. But do not quibble about insignificant matters. Also, he will usually ask you some question about your education, experience or your present job – partly to get you to start talking and to establish the interviewing "rapport." He may start the actual questioning, or turn it over to one of the other members. Frequently, each member undertakes the questioning on a particular area, one in which he is perhaps most competent, so you can expect each member to participate in the examination. Because time is limited, you may also expect some rather abrupt switches in the direction the questioning takes, so do not be upset by it. Normally, a board member will not pursue a single line of questioning unless he discovers a particular strength or weakness.

After each member has participated, the chairman will usually ask whether any member has any further questions, then will ask you if you have anything you wish to add. Unless you are expecting this question, it may floor you. Worse, it may start you off on an extended, extemporaneous speech. The board is not usually seeking more information. The question is principally to offer you a last opportunity to present further qualifications or to indicate that you have nothing to add. So, if you feel that a significant qualification or characteristic has been overlooked, it is proper to point it out in a sentence or so. Do not compliment the board on the thoroughness of their examination – they have been sketchy, and you know it. If you wish, merely say, "No thank you, I have nothing further to add." This is a point where you can "talk yourself out" of a good impression or fail to present an important bit of information. Remember, *you close the interview yourself*.

The chairman will then say, "That is all, Mr. _____, thank you." Do not be startled; the interview is over, and quicker than you think. Thank him, gather your belongings and take your leave. Save your sigh of relief for the other side of the door.

How to put your best foot forward

Throughout this entire process, you may feel that the board individually and collectively is trying to pierce your defenses, seek out your hidden weaknesses and embarrass and confuse you. Actually, this is not true. They are obliged to make an appraisal of your qualifications for the job you are seeking, and they want to see you in your best light. Remember, they must interview all candidates and a non-cooperative candidate may become a failure in spite of their best efforts to bring out his qualifications. Here are 15 suggestions that will help you:

1) Be natural – Keep your attitude confident, not cocky

If you are not confident that you can do the job, do not expect the board to be. Do not apologize for your weaknesses, try to bring out your strong points. The board is interested in a positive, not negative, presentation. Cockiness will antagonize any board member and make him wonder if you are covering up a weakness by a false show of strength.

2) Get comfortable, but don't lounge or sprawl

Sit erectly but not stiffly. A careless posture may lead the board to conclude that you are careless in other things, or at least that you are not impressed by the importance of the occasion. Either conclusion is natural, even if incorrect. Do not fuss with your clothing, a pencil or an ashtray. Your hands may occasionally be useful to emphasize a point; do not let them become a point of distraction.

3) Do not wisecrack or make small talk

This is a serious situation, and your attitude should show that you consider it as such. Further, the time of the board is limited – they do not want to waste it, and neither should you.

4) Do not exaggerate your experience or abilities

In the first place, from information in the application or other interviews and sources, the board may know more about you than you think. Secondly, you probably will not get away with it. An experienced board is rather adept at spotting such a situation, so do not take the chance.

5) If you know a board member, do not make a point of it, yet do not hide it

Certainly you are not fooling him, and probably not the other members of the board. Do not try to take advantage of your acquaintanceship – it will probably do you little good.

6) Do not dominate the interview

Let the board do that. They will give you the clues – do not assume that you have to do all the talking. Realize that the board has a number of questions to ask you, and do not try to take up all the interview time by showing off your extensive knowledge of the answer to the first one.

7) Be attentive

You only have 20 minutes or so, and you should keep your attention at its sharpest throughout. When a member is addressing a problem or question to you, give him your undivided attention. Address your reply principally to him, but do not exclude the other board members.

8) Do not interrupt

A board member may be stating a problem for you to analyze. He will ask you a question when the time comes. Let him state the problem, and wait for the question.

9) Make sure you understand the question

Do not try to answer until you are sure what the question is. If it is not clear, restate it in your own words or ask the board member to clarify it for you. However, do not haggle about minor elements.

10) Reply promptly but not hastily

A common entry on oral board rating sheets is "candidate responded readily," or "candidate hesitated in replies." Respond as promptly and quickly as you can, but do not jump to a hasty, ill-considered answer.

11) Do not be peremptory in your answers

A brief answer is proper – but do not fire your answer back. That is a losing game from your point of view. The board member can probably ask questions much faster than you can answer them.

12) Do not try to create the answer you think the board member wants

He is interested in what kind of mind you have and how it works – not in playing games. Furthermore, he can usually spot this practice and will actually grade you down on it.

13) Do not switch sides in your reply merely to agree with a board member

Frequently, a member will take a contrary position merely to draw you out and to see if you are willing and able to defend your point of view. Do not start a debate, yet do not surrender a good position. If a position is worth taking, it is worth defending.

14) Do not be afraid to admit an error in judgment if you are shown to be wrong

The board knows that you are forced to reply without any opportunity for careful consideration. Your answer may be demonstrably wrong. If so, admit it and get on with the interview.

15) Do not dwell at length on your present job

The opening question may relate to your present assignment. Answer the question but do not go into an extended discussion. You are being examined for a *new* job, not your present one. As a matter of fact, try to phrase ALL your answers in terms of the job for which you are being examined.

Basis of Rating

Probably you will forget most of these "do's" and "don'ts" when you walk into the oral interview room. Even remembering them all will not ensure you a passing grade. Perhaps you did not have the qualifications in the first place. But remembering them will help you to put your best foot forward, without treading on the toes of the board members.

Rumor and popular opinion to the contrary notwithstanding, an oral board wants you to make the best appearance possible. They know you are under pressure – but they also want to see how you respond to it as a guide to what your reaction would be under the pressures of the job you seek. They will be influenced by the degree of poise you display, the personal traits you show and the manner in which you respond.

ABOUT THIS BOOK

This book contains tests divided into Examination Sections. Go through each test, answering every question in the margin. We have also attached a sample answer sheet at the back of the book that can be removed and used. At the end of each test look at the answer key and check your answers. On the ones you got wrong, look at the right answer choice and learn. Do not fill in the answers first. Do not memorize the questions and answers, but understand the answer and principles involved. On your test, the questions will likely be different from the samples. Questions are changed and new ones added. If you understand these past questions you should have success with any changes that arise. Tests may consist of several types of questions. We have additional books on each subject should more study be advisable or necessary for you. Finally, the more you study, the better prepared you will be. This book is intended to be the last thing you study before you walk into the examination room. Prior study of relevant texts is also recommended. NLC publishes some of these in our Fundamental Series. Knowledge and good sense are important factors in passing your exam. Good luck also helps. So now study this Passbook, absorb the material contained within and take that knowledge into the examination. Then do your best to pass that exam.

EXAMINATION SECTION

EXAMINATION SECTION
TEST 1

DIRECTIONS: Each question or incomplete statement is followed by several suggested answers or completions. Select the one that BEST answers the question or completes the statement. *PRINT THE LETTER OF THE CORRECT ANSWER IN THE SPACE AT THE RIGHT.*

1. Of the following factors, which one is LEAST important in determining the size of staff needed in conducting an organization survey?
The

    A. effectiveness of the personnel in supplying data for the study
    B. extent of report writing anticipated
    C. number of field locations and headquarters staff units to be covered
    D. number of individuals to be interviewed as part of fact finding

2. In planning a systems survey, which one of the following is MOST important in carrying out an effective survey after the purpose and scope of the survey has been determined? The

    A. format of the survey report
    B. methods and techniques to be employed
    C. personality problems which may materialize
    D. exact starting and completion dates

3. Which of the following is the BEST way of organizing a final report?

    A. Begin and end the report with a summary of conclusions showing how conclusions were changed as a result of findings and recommendations
    B. Begin the report with an overall summary and then place findings and recommendations in several sections
    C. Intertwine findings and conclusions in such a manner as to make the report readable and interesting
    D. Place the findings and recommendations in separate sections avoiding conclusions to the maximum extent possible

4. Which of the following disadvantages is the MOST serious in making reports verbally rather than in writing?

    A. An effective analyst may not be a good public speaker.
    B. Verbal reports are conveniently forgotten.
    C. It may not generate actions and follow-through by recipients.
    D. There is a lack of permanent record to which one may later refer.

5. Following a management survey, which of the following represents the MOST serious pitfall which may be made in recommending improvements?

    A. Failure to convince people of the benefits to be derived from the recommendations
    B. Failure to freely discuss recommendations with those who must live with them
    C. Tendency of the survey team to put their own personalities into the report
    D. Tendency to deal in personalities instead of dealing with objectives and sound management practices

6. A working outline for management analysts should include all of the following EXCEPT

   A. a chronological outline of the work steps
   B. a determination of background information needed
   C. the distribution of outline to key staff and line personnel
   D. preliminary conclusions

7. Which one of the following areas is the MOST critical for an analyst during the fact-finding stage of a study?

   A. Accuracy of data appearing in reports
   B. Attitude of those being interviewed by the analyst
   C. Observations and tentative conclusions reached by the analyst
   D. Suggestions and recommendations of interviewees

8. Creating an organization embraces all of the following areas of management EXCEPT

   A. clarification of objectives
   B. determining the number of people required to man the organization
   C. establishing operating budgets to make the plan effective
   D. proper structuring of all key positions

9. In an organization, the MAJOR barrier to accepting change is the

   A. assumption by management that everyone will willingly accept change
   B. failure by management to present proposed changes in a proper fashion
   C. lack of adaptive abilities on the part of employees
   D. lack of understanding on the part of employees of sound management principles

10. A supervisor who wishes to attain established objectives should concentrate on

    A. determining whether management is operating at maximum effectiveness
    B. making suggestions for improving the organization
    C. planning work assignments
    D. securing salary increases for needy employees

11. A usually competent employee complains that he does not understand the procedures to be followed in performing a certain task although the supervisor has explained them twice and has demonstrated them.
    Of the following, the BEST course of action for the supervisor to take is to

    A. ask the employee whether he has any problems which are bothering him
    B. assign someone else to the job
    C. explain the procedures again and demonstrate at the same time
    D. have the employee perform the job while he watches and gives additional instructions

12. GENERALLY, in order to be completely qualified as a supervisor, a person

    A. should be able to perform exceptionally well at least one of the jobs he supervises and have some knowledge of the others
    B. must have an intimate working knowledge of all facets of the jobs which he supervises
    C. should know the basic principles and procedures of the jobs he supervises
    D. need know little or nothing of the jobs which he supervises as long as he knows the principles of supervision

13. Which of the following contributes MOST to the problem of waste and inefficiency in offices?

    A. Cost control is a budget function primarily.
    B. Most organizations do not have soundly conceived budgets.
    C. Procedures improvement staffs have not as yet gained acceptance among white-collar workers.
    D. Supervisors generally are uninterested in making improvements.

14. Which of the following contributes MOST to the great number of duplicate reports and double-checking procedures frequently found in offices?
    The

    A. desire for protection
    B. desire to improve problem solving
    C. intent to *manage by exception*
    D. need for budget data

15. Which one of the following BEST identifies the narrow technician as compared with the broad-gauged analyst?
    He

    A. analyzes the activities of an agency
    B. attempts to form sound relationships with departmental personnel
    C. focuses attention on forms design and appearance
    D. follows work flow from one bureau to another by charting operational steps

16. The percentage of budget funds allocated to fixed overhead costs can be MOST effectively reduced by

    A. a soundly conceived *promotion from within* policy
    B. increasing the amount of work performed
    C. relocating to areas closer to the center of cities
    D. tightening the *fixed cost* portion of the budget

17. The term *span of control* USUALLY refers to

    A. individuals reporting to a common supervisor
    B. individuals with whom one individual has contact in the course of performing his assigned duties
    C. levels of supervision in an organization
    D. percentage of time in an organization devoted to supervisory duties

18. For an analyst, which of the following is generally LEAST important in conducting a management survey?

    A. Ability of employees to understand goals of the survey
    B. Attitude of supervisors of employees
    C. Availability of employees for interviews
    D. Cooperation of employees

19. Of the following, morale in an agency is generally MOST significantly affected by

    A. agency policies and procedures
    B. agency recognition of executives supporting agency goals
    C. the extent to which an agency meets its announced goals
    D. the number of management surveys conducted in an agency

20. Which of the following BEST describes the principle of *management by exception?*

    A. Allocating executive time and effort in direct relation to the dollar values of the budget
    B. Decentralizing management and dealing primarily with problem areas
    C. Measuring only direct costs
    D. Setting goals and objectives and managing only these

21. A WEAKNESS of many budgetary systems today is that they

    A. are subjectively determined by those most directly involved
    B. focus on management weakness rather than management strength
    C. only show variable costs
    D. show in detail why losses are occurring

22. Standards on which budgets are developed should be based PRIMARILY on

    A. a general consensus   B. agency wishes
    C. analytical studies   D. historical performance

23. The income, cost, and expense goals making up a budget are aimed at achieving a pre-determined objective but do not necessarily measure the lowest possible costs. This is PRIMARILY so because

    A. budget committees are accounting-oriented and are not sympathetic with the supervisor's personnel problems
    B. budget committees fail to recognize the difference between direct and indirect costs
    C. the level of expenditures provided for in a budget by budget committees is frequently an arbitrary rather than a scientifically determined amount
    D. budget committees spend considerable time evaluating data to the point that the material gathered is not representative or current

24. Linear programming has all of the following characteristics EXCEPT: It
    A. is concerned with an optimum position in relation to some objective
    B. involves the selection among alternatives or the appropriate combination of alternatives
    C. not only requires that variables be qualitative but also rests on the assumption that the relations among the variables are minimized
    D. takes into account constraints or limits within which the decision is to be reached

25. In the PERT planning system, the time in which a non-critical task can slip schedule without holding up a project is USUALLY called
    A. constraint
    B. duration time
    C. dead time
    D. float or slack

26. The Produc-trol board and Schedugraphs are commercial variations of the _____ chart.
    A. flow
    B. Gantt
    C. layout
    D. multiple activity

27. The item which cannot be analyzed by such schematic techniques as the frequency polygon and the histogram is the
    A. age of accounts receivable
    B. morale and cohesiveness of work groups
    C. number of accidents in a plant
    D. wage pattern

28. An essential employee benefit of work measurement which FREQUENTLY is the key to the successful implementation of such a program is
    A. equitable work distribution
    B. facilitation of the development of budgets
    C. measurement and control of office productivity
    D. prevention of unfair work distribution

29. An organizational arrangement whereby different employees perform different work steps upon the same work items at the same time is called the _____ method.
    A. functional
    B. homogenous
    C. parallel or linear arrangement
    D. unit assembly

30. Frequently, opposition to a management survey stems from an executive's feeling that he might be considered responsible for the unsatisfactory conditions that the project is aimed at correcting.
    To overcome this type of opposition, the analyst should GENERALLY
    A. avoid the issue altogether
    B. face the situation *head on* and, if the executive is responsible, tell him so
    C. offer a reasonable explanation for those conditions early enough in the discussion to forestall any implication of criticism
    D. place the blame for the unsatisfactory conditions at the lowest level in the organization to avoid incriminating the boss

31. Which of the following situations is LEAST likely to require a management survey?

    A. Changes in policy
    B. Management requests for additional manpower
    C. Legislation mandating changes in operating procedures
    D. Significantly lower costs than anticipated

32. The efficiency of a procedure is often influenced by the practices or performance of departments that play no direct part in carrying it out.
    In view of this, the analyst must

    A. disregard the practices or performance of departments that play no direct part in the procedure
    B. do the very best job within the department studied to compensate for the outside problems
    C. ask for assistance in solving the problems created by this situation
    D. study and evaluate the external factors to the extent that they bear on the problem

33. Which one of the following is NOT a key step in staff delegation and development?

    A. Evaluation of the completed job
    B. Preparation of a subordinate to accept additional duties
    C. Review of daily progress
    D. Selection of a suitable job to be delegated

34. Which one of the following is NOT an essential characteristic of effective delegation?

    A. In delegating, the supervisor is no longer responsible.
    B. The individual to whom authority is delegated must be accountable for fulfillment of the task.
    C. The individual to whom authority is delegated must clearly understand this authority
    D. The individual to whom authority is delegated must get honest recognition for a job well done.

35. Whenever a manager must determine how long an operation should take, he is involved with the problem of setting a time standard.
    To PROPERLY set time standards, the manager must distinguish between

    A. estimation processes and evaluation processes
    B. performance of the slowest employee and performance of the fastest employee
    C. stop watch study and work sampling
    D. synthetic and arbitrary systems

36. Assuming a report is needed, which approach USUALLY facilitates implementation?
    A

    A. draft report submitted to key people for review, discussion, modification, and then resubmission in final form
    B. report in final form which sets forth alternate recommended solutions
    C. report which sets forth the problems and the recommended solution in conformance with the desires of those most directly involved
    D. visual presentation with minimal report writing

37. Of the following elements, which is the LEAST important in writing a survey report?
A

    A. definite course of action to be followed
    B. listing of benefits to be gained through implementation
    C. review of opinions as differentiated from facts
    D. summary of conclusions

38. Physical appearance and accuracy are important features in gaining acceptance to recommendations. Which one of the following might be OVERLOOKED in preparing a report which is to have wide distribution?

    A. A comprehensive index
    B. An attractive binder
    C. Proper spacing and page layout
    D. Charts and tables

39. The elimination of meaningless reports, although reducing the total information output, IMPROVES the management process by

    A. determining the number of employees required to perform the work assigned
    B. identifying the difference between direct and indirect costs
    C. increasing the effectiveness of executives
    D. limiting the budget to variable costs

40. In determining whether or not to use a computerized system as opposed to a manual system, which of the following would normally have the MOST influence on the decision?
The

    A. availability of analysts and programmers to design and install the system
    B. availability of computer time
    C. basic premise that all computerized systems are superior to manual systems
    D. volume and complexity of transactions required

KEY (CORRECT ANSWERS)

1. A	11. D	21. A	31. D
2. B	12. C	22. C	32. D
3. B	13. C	23. C	33. C
4. D	14. A	24. C	34. A
5. D	15. C	25. D	35. A
6. D	16. B	26. B	36. A
7. C	17. A	27. B	37. C
8. C	18. A	28. A	38. B
9. B	19. A	29. D	39. C
10. C	20. B	30. C	40. D

TEST 2

DIRECTIONS: Each question or incomplete statement is followed by several suggested answers or completions. Select the one that BEST answers the question or completes the statement. *PRINT THE LETTER OF THE CORRECT ANSWER IN THE SPACE AT THE RIGHT*

1. The one of the following that is NOT normally involved in the development of a management information system is

   A. determination of the best method of preparing and presenting the required information
   B. determination of line and staff relationships within the various units of the organizational structure
   C. determination of what specific information is needed for decision-making and control
   D. identification of the critical aspects of the business, i.e., the end results and other elements of performance which need to be planned and controlled

2. The long-term growth in size and complexity of both business and government has increased management's dependence on more formal written summaries of operating results in place of the informal, on-the-spot observations and judgments of smaller organizations.
   In addition, there is a growing management need to

   A. increase the complexity of those phases of the management process which have previously been simplified
   B. increase the speed and accuracy of artificial intelligence
   C. measure the effectiveness of managerial performance
   D. reduce alcoholism by greatly limiting personal contacts between the various levels of management within the organization

3. Of the following, it is MOST essential that a management information system provide information needed for

   A. determining computer time requirements
   B. developing new office layouts
   C. drawing new organization charts
   D. planning and measuring results

4. The PRIMARY purpose of control reports is to

   A. compare actual performance with planned results
   B. determine staffing requirements
   C. determine the work flow
   D. develop a new budget

5. Which one of the following has the GREATEST negative impact on communications in a large organization?

   A. Delays in formulating variable policies relating to communications
   B. Failure to conduct comprehensive courses in communications skills
   C. Failure to get information to those who need it
   D. Unclear organizational objectives

6. Efficiency of an organization is significantly impacted by all of the following EXCEPT

    A. network connectivity
    B. software compatibility
    C. hardware upgrades
    D. cloud data storage

7. The type of computer configuration in which the data are processed at one time after they have been made a matter of record is known as

    A. batching   B. in line   C. off line   D. real time

8. A computer configuration system in which the input or output equipment is directly connected and operates under control of the computer is known as

    A. off line
    B. on line
    C. random access
    D. real time

9. A manager who wants to quickly analyze the output of a particular department would most likely refer to which one of the following?

    A. An Excel spreadsheet with production data logged by department
    B. Email reports submitted by department leaders
    C. Quarterly reports describing production targets and measurements
    D. An Excel spreadsheet with employee-generated survey data related to typical daily output and capabilities

10. Computers are generally considered to consist of four major sections. The one of the following which is NOT a major section is

    A. buffer
    B. control
    C. processing
    D. storage

11. Of the following, administrative control is PRIMARILY dependent upon

    A. adequate information
    B. a widespread spy network
    C. strict supervisors
    D. strong sanctions

12. Meticulous care must be exercised in writing the methodology section of the research report so that

    A. another investigator will achieve the same results if he repeats the study
    B. the interpretation of the findings cannot be challenged
    C. the report will be well balanced
    D. the rules of scientific logic are clearly indicated

13. When data are grouped into a frequency distribution, the *true mode* by definition is the _____ in the distribution.

    A. 50% point
    B. largest single range
    C. point of greatest concentration
    D. smallest single range

14. Which of the following is LEAST likely to be a potential benefit arising from the use of electronic data processing systems?

    A. Analysis of more data and analysis of data in greater depth than manual systems
    B. Increased speed and accuracy in information processing
    C. Lower capital expenditures for office equipment
    D. Reduced personnel costs in tabulating and reporting functions

15. A *grapevine* is BEST defined as

    A. a harmful method of communication
    B. a system of communication operative below the executive level
    C. an informal communication system of no functional importance to an organization
    D. the internal and non-systematic channel of communication within an organization

16. Of the following, the symbol shown at the right, as used in a systems flow chart, means

    A. document
    B. manual operation
    C. planning
    D. process

17. The mean age of a sample group drawn from population X is 37.5 years and the standard error of the mean is 5.9. There is a *99%* probability that the computed mean age of other samples drawn from population X would fall within the range of

    A. 31.6–43.4   B. 26.0–52.7
    C. 22.2–52.8   D. 20.0–55.0

18. After a budget has been developed, it serves to

    A. assist the accounting department in posting expenditures
    B. measure the effectiveness of department managers
    C. provide a yardstick against which actual costs are measured
    D. provide the operating department with total expenditures to date

19. In order to ensure that work measurement or time study results will be consistent from one study to another, and reflect a fair day's work, the performance of the clerks must be rated or levelled.
    Which of the following is LEAST likely to be included among the techniques for determining the performance level or for rating the study?

    A. Predetermined times   B. Published rating tables
    C. Sampling studies   D. Training films

20. Of the following, the BEST practice to follow when training a new employee is to

    A. encourage him to feel free to ask questions at any time
    B. immediately demonstrate how fast his job can be done so he will know what is expected of him
    C. let him watch other employees for a week or two
    D. point out mistakes after completion so he will learn by experience

21. An IMPORTANT aspect to keep in mind during the decision-making process is that

    A. all possible alternatives for attaining goals should be sought out and considered
    B. considering various alternatives only leads to confusion
    C. once a decision has been made, it cannot be retracted
    D. there is only one correct method to reach any goal

22. Implementation of accountability REQUIRES

    A. a leader who will not hesitate to take punitive action
    B. an established system of communication from the bottom to the top
    C. explicit directives from leaders
    D. too much expense to justify it

23. Of the following, the MAJOR difference between systems and procedures analysis and work simplification is:

    A. The former complicates organizational routine and the latter simplifies it
    B. The former is objective and the latter is subjective
    C. The former generally utilizes expert advice and the latter is a *do-it-yourself* improvement by supervisors and workers
    D. There is no difference other than in name

24. Systems development is concerned with providing

    A. a specific set of work procedures
    B. an overall framework to describe general relationships
    C. definitions of particular organizational functions
    D. organizational symbolism

25. Organizational systems and procedures should be

    A. developed as problems arise as no design can anticipate adequately the requirements of an organization
    B. developed jointly by experts in systems and procedures and the people who are responsible for implementing them
    C. developed solely by experts in systems and procedures
    D. eliminated whenever possible to save unnecessary expense

26. The CHIEF danger of a decentralized control system is that

    A. excessive reports and communications will be generated
    B. problem areas may not be detected readily
    C. the expense will become prohibitive
    D. this will result in too many *chiefs*

27. Of the following, management guides and controls clerical work PRINCIPALLY through

    A. close supervision and constant checking of personnel
    B. spot checking of clerical procedures
    C. strong sanctions for clerical supervisors
    D. the use of printed forms

28. Which of the following is MOST important before conducting fact-finding interviews?

    A. Becoming acquainted with all personnel to be interviewed
    B. Explaining the techniques you plan to use
    C. Explaining to the operating officials the purpose and scope of the study
    D. Orientation of the physical layout

29. Of the following, the one that is NOT essential in carrying out a comprehensive work improvement program is

    A. standards of performance
    B. supervisory training
    C. work count/task list
    D. work distribution chart

30. Which of the following control techniques is MOST useful on large, complex systems projects?

    A. A general work plan
    B. Gantt chart
    C. Monthly progress report
    D. PERT chart

31. The action which is MOST effective in gaining acceptance of a study by the agency which is being studied is

    A. a directive from the agency head to install a study based on recommendations included in a report
    B. a lecture-type presentation following approval of the procedures
    C. a written procedure in narrative form covering the proposed system with visual presentations and discussions
    D. procedural charts showing the *before* situation, forms, steps, etc. to the employees affected

32. Which of the following is NOT an advantage in the use of oral instructions as compared with written instructions? Oral instruction(s)

    A. can easily be changed
    B. is superior in transmitting complex directives
    C. facilitate exchange of information between a superior and his subordinate
    D. with discussions make it easier to ascertain understanding

33. Which organization principle is MOST closely related to procedural analysis and improvement?

    A. Duplication, overlapping, and conflict should be eliminated.
    B. Managerial authority should be clearly defined.
    C. The objectives of the organization should be clearly defined.
    D. Top management should be freed of burdensome detail.

34. Which one of the following is the MAJOR objective of operational audits?

    A. Detecting fraud
    B. Determining organization problems
    C. Determining the number of personnel needed
    D. Recommending opportunities for improving operating and management practices

35. Of the following, the formalization of organization structure is BEST achieved by
    A. a narrative description of the plan of organization
    B. functional charts
    C. job descriptions together with organization charts
    D. multi-flow charts

36. Budget planning is MOST useful when it achieves
    A. cost control
    B. forecast of receipts
    C. performance review
    D. personnel reduction

37. The UNDERLYING principle of sound administration is to
    A. base administration on investigation of facts
    B. have plenty of resources available
    C. hire a strong administrator
    D. establish a broad policy

38. Although questionnaires are not the best survey tool the management analyst has to use, there are times when a good questionnaire can expedite the *fact-finding* phase of a management survey.
    Which of the following should be AVOIDED in the design and distribution of the questionnaire?
    A. Questions should be framed so that answers can be classified and tabulated for analysis.
    B. Those receiving the questionnaire must be knowledgeable enough to accurately provide the information desired.
    C. The questionnaire should enable the respondent to answer in a narrative manner.
    D. The questionnaire should require a minimum amount of writing.

39. Of the following, the formula which is used to calculate the arithmetic mean from data grouped in a frequency distribution is:
    M =

    A. $\dfrac{n}{\Sigma fx}$
    B. $N(\Sigma fx)$
    C. $\dfrac{\Sigma fx}{N}$
    D. $\dfrac{\Sigma x}{fN}$

40. Arranging large groups of numbers in frequency distributions
    A. gives a more composite picture of the total group than a random listing
    B. is misleading in most cases
    C. is unnecessary in most instances
    D. presents the data in a form whereby further manipulation of the group is eliminated

KEY (CORRECT ANSWERS)

1. B	11. A	21. A	31. C
2. C	12. A	22. B	32. B
3. D	13. C	23. C	33. A
4. A	14. C	24. B	34. D
5. C	15. D	25. B	35. C
6. C	16. B	26. B	36. A
7. A	17. C	27. D	37. A
8. B	18. C	28. C	38. C
9. A	19. C	29. B	39. C
10. A	20. A	30. D	40. A

EXAMINATION SECTION
TEST 1

DIRECTIONS: Each question or incomplete statement is followed by several suggested answers or completions. Select the one that BEST answers the question or completes the statement. *PRINT THE LETTER OF THE CORRECT ANSWER IN THE SPACE AT THE RIGHT.*

1. With a management staff of 15 capable analysts, which of the following organizational approaches would generally be BEST for overall results? Organization
   A. by specialists in fields, such as management, organization, systems analysis
   B. by clientele to be served, such as hospitals, police education, social services
   C. where all 15 report directly to head of the management staff
   D. by specialized study groups with flexibility in assigning staff under a qualified project leader

2. In conducting a general management survey to identify problems and opportunities, which of the following would it be LEAST necessary to consider?
   A. Identifying program and planning deficiencies in each functional area
   B. Organization problems
   C. Sound management practices not being used
   D. The qualifications of the supervisory personnel

3. Which of the following statements MOST accurately defines *operations research*?
   A. A highly sophisticated system used in the analysis of management problems
   B. A specialized application of electronic data processing in the analysis of management problems
   C. Research on operating problems
   D. The application of sophisticated mathematical tools to the analysis of management problems

4. Theoretically, an ideal organization structure can be set up for each enterprise. In actual practice, the ideal organization structure is seldom, if ever, obtained. Of the following, the one that is of LEAST influence in determining the organization structure is the
   A. existence of agreements and favors among members of the organization
   B. funds available
   C. growing trend of management to discard established forms in favor of new forms
   D. opinions and beliefs of top executives

5. To which one of the following is it MOST important that the functional or technical staff specialist in a large organization devote major attention?
   A. Conducting audits of line operations
   B. Controlling of people in the line organization
   C. Developing improve approaches, plans, and procedures and assisting the line organization in their implementation
   D. Providing advice to his superior and to operating units

5.____

6. In the planning for reorganization of a department, which one of the following principles relating to the assignment of functions is NOT correct?
   A. Line and staff functions should be separated.
   B. Separate functions should be assigned to separate organizational units.
   C. There should be no disturbance of the previously assigned tasks of personnel.
   D. There should generally be no overlapping among organizational elements.

6.____

7. Results are BEST accomplished within an organization when the budgets and plans are developed by the
   A. budget office, independent of the operating units
   B. head of the operating unit based on analysis of prior year's operations after discussion with his superior
   C. head of the operating unit with general guidelines and data from higher authority and the budget office, and input from key personnel
   D. head of the organization unit based on an analysis of prior year's operations

7.____

8. The *management process* is a term used to describe the responsibilities common to
   A. all levels of management   B. first-line supervisors
   C. middle management jobs   D. top management jobs

8.____

9. Of the following, committees are BEST used for
   A. advising the head of the organization
   B. improving functional work
   C. making executive decisions
   D. making specific planning decisions

9.____

10. Which of the following would NOT be a part of a management control system?
    A. An objective test of new ideas or methods in operation
    B. Determination of need for organization improvement
    C. Objective comparison of operating results
    D. Provision of information useful for revising objectives, programs, and operations

10.____

11. Of the following, the one which a line role generally does NOT include is
    A. controlling results and performance
    B. coordination work and exchanging ideas with other line organizations
    C. implementation of approved plans developed by staff
    D. planning work and making operation decisions

12. In a normal curve, one standard deviation would include MOST NEARLY what percentage of the cases involved?
    A. 50%   B. 68%   C. 95%   D. 99%

13. The Office Layout Chart is a sketch of the physical arrangements of the office to which has been added the flow lines of the principal work performed there. Which one of the following states the BEST advantage of superimposing the work flow onto the desk layout?
    A. Lighting and acoustics can be improved.
    B. Line and staff relationships can be determined.
    C. Obvious misarrangements can be corrected.
    D. The number of delays can be determined.

14. An advantage of the Multiple Process Chart over the Flow Process Chart is that the Multiple Process Chart shows the
    A. individual worker's activity
    B. number of delays
    C. sequence of operations
    D. simultaneous flow of work in several departments

15. Of the following, which is the MAJOR advantage of a microfilm record retention system?
    A. Filing can follow the terminal digit system.
    B. Retrieving documents from the files is faster.
    C. Significant space is saved in storing records.
    D. To read a microfilm record, a film reader is not necessary.

16. Which one of the following questions should the management analyst generally consider FIRST?
    A. How is it being done? and Why should it be done that way?
    B. What is being done? and Why is it necessary?
    C. When should this job be done? and What should he do it?
    D. Who should do the job? and Why should he do it?

17. Assume that you are in the process of eliminating unnecessary forms. The answer to which one of the following questions would be LEAST relevant?
    A. Could the information be obtained elsewhere?
    B. Is the form properly designed?
    C. Is the form used as intended?
    D. Is the purpose of the form essential to the operation?

18. Use of color in forms adds to their cost. Sometimes, however, the use of color will greatly simplify procedure and more than pay for itself in time saved and errors eliminated.
    This is ESPECIALLY true when
    A. a form passes through many reviewers
    B. considerable sorting is required
    C. the form is other than a standard size
    D. the form will not be sent through the mail

18.____

19. Of the following techniques, the one GENERALLY employed and considered BEST in forms design is to divide writing lines into boxes with captions printed in small type _____ of the box.
    A. centered in the lower part
    B. centered in the upper part
    C. in the upper left-hand corner
    D. in the lower right-hand corner

19.____

20. Many forms authorities advocate the construction of a functional forms file or index.
    If such a file is set up, the MOST effective way of classifying forms for such an index is classification by
    A. department
    B. form number
    C. name or type of form
    D. subject to which the form applies

20.____

21. An interrelated pattern of jobs which makes up the structure of a system is known as
    A. a chain of command
    B. cybernetics
    C. the formal organization
    D. the maintenance pattern

21.____

22. A transparent sheet of film containing multiple rows of microimages is characteristic of which one of the following types of microfilm?
    A. Aperture
    B. Jacket
    C. Microfiche
    D. Roll or reel

22.____

23. PRIMARY responsibility for training and development of employees generally rests with
    A. outside training agencies
    B. the individual who needs training
    C. the line supervisor
    D. the training specialist in the Personnel Office

23.____

24. Which of the following approaches usually provides the BEST communication in the objectives and values of a new program which is to be introduced?
    A. A general written description of the program by the program manager for review by those who share responsibility
    B. An effective verbal presentation by the program manager to those affected
    C. Development of the plan and operational approach in carrying out the program by the program manager assisted by his key subordinates
    D. Development of the plan by the program manager's supervisor

24.____

25. The term *total systems concept*, as used in electronic data processing, refers   25.____
    A. only to the computer and its associated electronic accessories
    B. only o the paper information output, or *software* aspect
    C. to a large computer-based information handling system, which supplies the information needs of an entire agency or corporation
    D. to all of the automated and manual information systems in a specific subdivision of an organization

26. Of the following, scientific management can BEST be considered as an attempt   26.____
    to establish work procedures
    A. in fields of scientific endeavors
    B. which are beneficial only to bosses
    C. which require less control
    D. utilizing the concept of a man-machine system

27. The MAJOR failing of efficiency engineering was that it   27.____
    A. overlooked the human factor
    B. required experts to implement the techniques
    C. was not based on true scientific principles
    D. was too costly and time consuming

28. Which of the following organizations is MOST noted throughout the world for   28.____
    its training in management?
    A. American Management Association
    B. American Political Science Association
    C. Society for the Advancement of Management
    D. Systems and Procedures Association

29. The GENERAL method of arriving at program objectives should be   29.____
    A. a trial and error process
    B. developed as the program progresses
    C. included in the program plan
    D. left to the discretion of the immediate supervisors

30. The review and appraisal of an organization to determine waste and deficiencies,   30.____
    improved methods, better means of control, more efficient operations, and
    greater use of human and physical facilities is known as a(n)
    A. management audit   B. manpower survey
    C. work simplification   D. operations audit

31. When data are grouped into a frequency distribution, the *median* is BEST   31.____
    defined as the _____ in the distribution.
    A. 50% point   B. largest single range
    C. smallest single range   D. point of greatest concentration

32. The manual, visual, and mental elements into which an operation may be   32.____
    analyzed in time and motion study are denoted by the term
    A. measurement   B. positioning   C. standards   D. therbligs

33. Of the following, the symbol shown at the right, as used in a systems flow chart, denotes
    A. decision
    B. document
    C. manual operation
    D. process

33.____

34. Of the following agencies of city government, the one with the LARGEST expense budget for the current fiscal year is the
    A. environmental protection administration
    B. department of social services
    C. municipal service administration
    D. police department

34.____

35. A feasibility study is the first phase in the process of conversion from manual to computerized data processing.
    The phases, in sequence, are the feasibility study, system
    A. conversion, system installation, follow up
    B. design, installation
    C. design, follow up, installation
    D. design, system conversion, installation

35.____

36.

The type of chart illustrated above is generally known as a _____ Chart.
    A. Flow   B. Gantt
    C. Work Simplification   D. Motion-Time Study

36.____

37.

37.____

The type of chart illustrated on the previous page is generally known as a _____ Chart.
   A. Flow
   B. Gantt
   C. Simo
   D. Work Simplification

38. 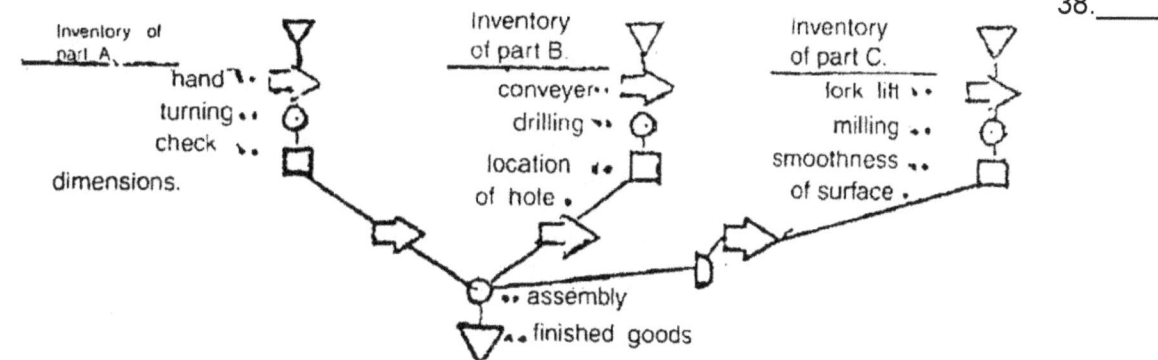 38.____

The type of chart illustrated above is generally known as a(n) _____ Chart.
   A. Multiple Activity
   B. Motion-Time
   C. Work Place Layout
   D. Operation Process

39. 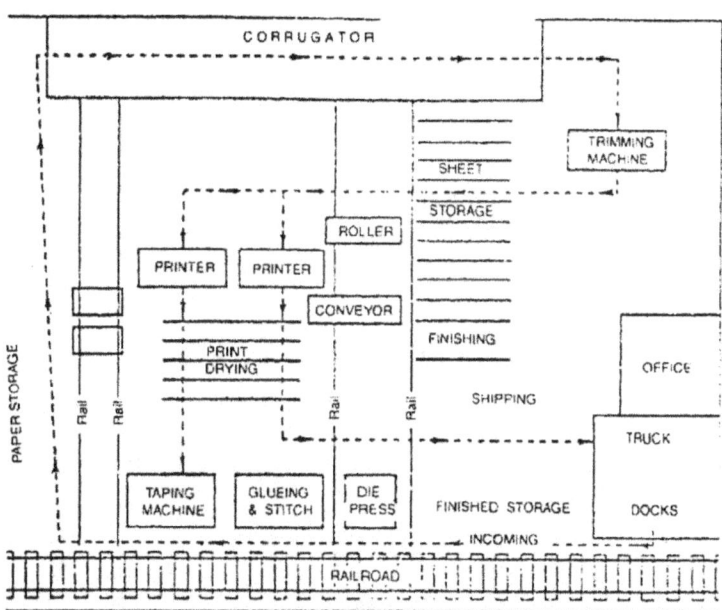 39.____

The one illustrated above is generally known as a
   A. Gantt Chart
   B. Multiple Activity Chart
   C. Planned Flow Diagram
   D. Work Place Diagram

40.

[chart image]

The type of chart illustrated above is generally known as a(n) _____ Chart.
A. Analysis
B. Flow Process
C. Man or Material
D. Multiple Activity

KEY (CORRECT ANSWERS)

1.	D	11.	B	21.	C	31.	A
2.	D	12.	B	22.	C	32.	D
3.	D	13.	C	23.	C	33.	A
4.	C	14.	D	24.	C	34.	B
5.	C	15.	C	25.	C	35.	D
6.	C	16.	B	26.	D	36.	B
7.	C	17.	B	27.	A	37.	C
8.	A	18.	B	28.	A	38.	D
9.	A	19.	C	29.	C	39.	C
10.	B	20.	D	30.	A	40.	B

TEST 2

DIRECTIONS: Each question or incomplete statement is followed by several suggested answers or completions. Select the one that BEST answers the question or completes the statement. *PRINT THE LETTER OF THE CORRECT ANSWER IN THE SPACE AT THE RIGHT.*

1. The one of the following which is MOST important in getting a systems survey off to a good start is
    A. a kick-off meeting with key personnel covering the purpose of the study and introduction of the survey staff
    B. a prior knowledge of the organization manual, charts, and statement of responsibility
    C. knowledge of personality problems in the agency needing special attention
    D. written announcement from the agency head

2. Which of the following is the LEAST important factor in planning an administrative survey?
    A. Developing a work plan and time schedule
    B. Knowledge of sound organization concepts and principles
    C. Survey techniques and methods to be used for analysis in compiling data needed
    D. The purpose, scope, and level of the survey

3. Assume that a supervisor, when reviewing a decision reached by one of his subordinates, finds the decision incorrect.
   Under these circumstances, it would be MOST desirable for the supervisor to
    A. correct the decision and inform the subordinate of this at a staff meeting
    B. correct the decision and suggest a more detailed analysis in the future
    C. help the employee find the reason for the correct decision
    D. refrain from assigning this type of problem to the employee

4. After an analyst has identified a problem area, which one of the following is the MOST important step in getting management to recognize that a problem does exist?
    A. A brief statement describing the problem
    B. Implications if problem is not corrected
    C. Relationship to other problems
    D. Supporting factual evidence and data indicating that the problem does exist

5. The statement, *work expands to fit the time available for its completion*, refers MOST directly to
    A. job enlargement principles
    B. Parkinson's Law
    C. The Open System Theory
    D. The Peter Principle

6. A comprehensive and constructive examination of a company, institution, or branch of government, or of any of its components such as an agency, division, or department, and its plans and objectives, methods of control, its means of operations, and its use of human and physical facilities is COMMONLY known as a(n) _____ audit.
   A. systems
   B. extensive financial
   C. operational or management
   D. organizational

6.____

7. Assume you are assigned to analyze the details of the procedures a clerk follows in order to complete filling out an invoice or a requisition. Your purpose is to simplify and shorten the procedure he has been trained to use.
   The MOST appropriate chart for this purpose would be the
   A. block flow diagram
   B. flow process chart
   C. forms flow chart
   D. work distribution chart

7.____

8. In identifying problems and opportunities for improvement, which one of the following is MOST closely related to organization planning?
   A. Effective operating procedures issued from headquarters
   B. Effective records management
   C. Need for improved management concepts and practices
   D. Review of the salary and wage administration program

8.____

9. MOST of the working time of the functional or technical staff specialist in a large organization should be focused on
   A. conducting audits of line operations
   B. developing improved approaches, plans, and procedures and assisting the line organization in their implementation
   C. providing advice to his superior and to operating units
   D. the number of people in the line organization

9.____

10. The LEAST effective way for a survey group to plan is to
    A. clarify objectives and identify problems
    B. conduct planning and review sessions annually when budgets are prepared
    C. periodically conduct review sessions for purposes of coordination
    D. undertake specific action programs

10.____

11. Which one of the following is the MOST important element of a good manpower plan?
    A. Establishing inventories of capable personnel
    B. Forecasting the number of people needed in the future
    C. Having the right people for all jobs when needed
    D. Identifying training needs

11.____

12. Completed staff work is MOST effective in accomplishing which one of the following?
    A. Determination of the problems of the line organization
    B. Determination of the staffing needs of an organization

12.____

C. Preparation of effective proposals and approaches to improve fine results
D. Review of budgets proposed by line organization

13. What generally is the PRINCIPAL objection to the use of form letters? 13.____
The
   A. difficulty of developing a form letter to serve the purpose
   B. excessive time involved in selecting the proper form letter
   C. errors in selecting form letters
   D. impersonality of form letters

14. What is the BEST approach for introducing change? 14.____
A
   A. combination of written and also verbal communication to all personnel affected by the change
   B. general bulletin to all personnel
   C. meeting pointing out all the values of the new approach
   D. written directive to key personnel

15. The FIRST step in designing an effective management survey is 15.____
   A. examining backlogs   B. flow charting
   C. motion analysis and time study   D. project planning

16. In statistical sampling, the error which will NOT be exceeded by 50 percent 16.____
of the cases is known as the
   A. difference between two means   B. probable error
   C. standard deviation   D. standard error of the mean

17. In a normal or bell-shaped curve, the area encompassed by two standard 17.____
deviations from the mean is
   A. 68%   B. 95%   C. 97%   D. 99%

18. The statistical average referring to that point on the scale at which the 18.____
concentration is greatest or that value which occurs the greatest number of
times and which might be taken as typical of the entire distribution is called the
   A. mean   B. median   C. mode   D. quartile

19. In process charting, the symbol which is used when conditions (except those 19.____
which intentionally change the physical or chemical characteristics of the
object) do not permit or require immediate performance is
   A. □   B. ○   C. D   D. ▽

20. Assume that you are making a study of a central headquarters office which 20.____
processes claims received from a number of district offices. You notice the
following problems: Some employees are usually busy, while others doing the
same kind of work in the same grade have little to do, high level professional
people frequently spend considerable time searching for files in the file room.

Which of the following charts would be MOST useful to record and analyze the data needed to help solve these problems?
_____ Chart.
A. Forms Distribution
B. Process
C. Space Layout
D. Work Distribution

21. Which of the following types of work would NOT be readily measured by conventional time study techniques?
Work
A. of sufficient volume, uniform in nature, that will justify the cost of continuing and maintaining controls
B. that is countable in precise quantitative terms
C. that is essentially creative and considerably varied in content
D. that is repetitive, uniform, and homogeneous in content over a period of time

22. Which of the following should be the FIRST consideration in a work simplification study?
Can the
A. sequence be changed for improvement?
B. task be combined with another?
C. task be eliminated
D. task be simplified?

23. In evaluating the sequence of operations involved in the clerical processing, which of the items listed below would be an indicator that methods improvements are needed?
A. Some operations duplicate previous operations.
B. The supervisor believes many of the company's policies are wrong.
C. There is a high turnover of mail clerks.
D. Work is logged into and out of the department.

24. Of the following, the one that is MOST likely to make a methods change unacceptable is when the
A. change does not threaten the workers' security
B. change follows a series of previously unsuccessful similar changes
C. change has been well thought out and properly introduced
D. people affected by the change have participated in the development of the changes

25. Which of the following questions has the LEAST significant bearing on the analysis of the paperwork flow?
A. How is the work brought into the department and how is it taken away?
B. How many workstations are involved in processing the work within the department?
C. Is the work received and removed in the proper quantity?
D. Where is the supervisor's desk located in relationship to those he supervises?

26. Which of the following does NOT have significant bearing on the arrangement, sequence, and zoning of information into box captions?
The
   A. layout of the source documents from which the information is taken
   B. logical flow of data
   C. needs of forms to be prepared from this form
   D. type of print to be employed

26.____

27. In determining the spacing requirements of a form and the size of the boxes to be used, PRIMARY consideration should be given to the
   A. distribution of the form
   B. method of entry, i.e., handwritten or machine and type of machine
   C. number of copies
   D. number of items to be entered

27.____

28. Of the following, the BEST technique to follow when providing instructions for the completion and routing of a form is to _____ the form.
   A. imprint the instructions on the face of
   B. imprint the instructions on the back of
   C. provide a written procedure to accompany
   D. provide verbal instructions when issuing

28.____

29. A forms layout style where a separate space in the shape of a box is provided for each item of information requested and the caption or question for each item is shown in the upper left-hand corner of each box is known as the _____ style.
   A. box
   B. checkbox
   C. checklist
   D. checkbox and checklist

29.____

30. It is the office manager's responsibility to promote office safety and eliminate hazards. A number of policies and procedures are widely advocated and followed by management and safety experts.
Of the following, the policy or procedure that is LEAST valid is:
   A. Each department supervisor should be required to complete a report at the time of each accident so that the person in charge of safety administration will be able to analyze the pattern of common causes and improve safety conditions.
   B. Electrical cords and connectors for machines and equipment should be routinely checked so as to eliminate fire and shock hazards.
   C. Employees should be informed of the type of accidents which may occur
   D. Smoking at desks should be prohibited so as to avoid the possibility of fire hazards; and a lounge provided for this purpose.

30.____

31. An effective discussion leader is one who
   A. announces the problem and his preconceived solution at the start of the discussion
   B. guides and directs the discussion according to pre-arranged outline
   C. interrupts or corrects confused participants to save time
   D. permits anyone to say anything at anytime

31.____

32. Under what circumstances would it be MOST advisable to have two or more clerks in a department share the same adding machine?
When
   A. capital appropriations are tight
   B. the clerks sharing the adding machine are located at adjacent desks
   C. the clerks sharing the adding machine get along with one another
   D. the need for the equipment is so little that there is negligible time lost in sharing the adding machine

33. Of the following, the statement that is MOST descriptive of, and fundamental to, proper office landscaping is:
   A. All clerical desks should be arranged singly and in rows
   B. The layout should be built around the flow of information and work in the office.
   C. The layout should be built around the recognized organizational hierarchy of the office unit.
   D. There should be many planters arranged to give the office an open look.

34. The MOST significant factor to be considered in deciding on upgrades to clerical-related software is
   A. reduction of costs
   B. standardization of software across all departments
   C. availability of new and innovative features
   D. compatibility and efficiency related to clerical tasks

35. The human relations movement in management theory is BASICALLY concerned with
   A. counteracting employee unrest
   B. eliminating the *time and motion* man
   C. interrelationships among individuals in organizations
   D. the psychology of the worker

36. PERT, as commonly used, stood for
   A. Periodic Estimate of Resource Trends
   B. Potential Energy Research Technology
   C. Professional Engineer Review Tests
   D. Program Evaluation and Review Technique

37. The BEST type of chart to use in showing the absolute movement or change of a continuous series of data over a period of time, such as changes in prices, employment, or expenses, is usually a _____ chart.
   A. bar   B. line   C. multiple bar   D. pie

38. Software designed for statistical record keeping and organization is called
   A. Navigator   B. Acrobat   C. Outlook   D. Excel

39. Due to its size, a tablet (ex. iPad) has ____ than a standard office computer. 39.____
    A. less reliability
    B. less computing power
    C. more functionality
    D. none of the above

40. Of the following, the one theme that has NOT had an elevated impact on computing and business in the 2020s is 40.____
    A. free unlimited access to email
    B. advanced mobile technology
    C. developments in artificial intelligence (AI)
    D. automation of service tasks

KEY (CORRECT ANSWERS)

1.	A	11.	C	21.	C	31.	B
2.	B	12.	C	22.	C	32.	D
3.	C	13.	D	23.	A	33.	B
4.	D	14.	A	24.	B	34.	D
5.	B	15.	D	25.	D	35.	C
6.	C	16.	B	26.	D	36.	D
7.	B	17.	B	27.	B	37.	B
8.	C	18.	C	28.	A	38.	D
9.	B	19.	C	29.	A	39.	D
10.	B	20.	D	30.	D	40.	A

EXAMINATION SECTION
TEST 1

DIRECTIONS: Each question or incomplete statement is followed by several suggested answers or completions. Select the one that BEST answers the question or completes the statement. *PRINT THE LETTER OF THE CORRECT ANSWER IN THE SPACE AT THE RIGHT.*

1. An executive assigns A, the head of a staff unit, to devise plans for reducing the delay in submittal of reports by a local agency headed by C. The reports are under the supervision of C's subordinate line official B with whom A is to deal directly. In his investigation, A finds: (1) the reasons for the delay; and (2) poor practices which have either been overlooked or condoned by line official B.
   Of the following courses of action A could take, the BEST one would be to
   A. develop recommendations with line official B with regard to reducing the delay and correcting the poor practice and then report fully to his own executive
   B. discuss the findings with C in an attempt to correct the situation before making any formal report on the poor practices
   C. report both findings to his executive, attaching the explanation offered by C
   D. report to his executive on the first finding and discuss the second in a friendly way with line official B
   E. report the first finding to his executive, ignoring the second until his opinion is requested

1.____

2. Drafts of a proposed policy, prepared by a staff committee, are circulated to ten member of the field staff of the organization by route slips with a request for comments within two weeks. Two members of the field staff make extensive comments, four offer editorial suggestions, and the remainder make minor favorable comments. Shortly after, it found that the statement needs considerable revision by the field staff.
   Of the following possible reasons for the original failure of the field staff to identify difficulties, the MOST likely is that the
   A. field staff did not take sufficient time to review the manual
   B. field staff had not been advised of the type of contribution expected
   C. low morale of the field staff prevented their showing interest
   D. policy statement was too advanced for the staff
   E. staff committee was not sufficiently representative

2.____

3. Operator participation in management improvement work is LEAST likely to
   A. assure the use of best available management technique
   B. overcome the stigma of the outside expert
   C. place responsibility for improvement in the person who knows the job best
   D. simplify installation
   E. take advantage of the desire of most operators to seek self-improvement

3.____

4. In general, the morale of workers in an agency is MOST frequently and MOST significantly affected by the
   A. agency policies of organizational structure and operational procedures
   B. distance of the employee's job from his home community
   C. fringe benefits
   D. number of opportunities for advancement
   E. relationship with supervisors

5. Of the following, the PRIMARY function of a work distribution chart is to
   A. analyze the soundness of existing divisions of labor
   B. eliminate the unnecessary clerical detail
   C. establish better supervisory techniques
   D. simplify work methods
   E. weed out core functions

6. In analyzing a process chart, which one of the following should be asked FIRST?
   A. How B. When C. Where D. Who E. Why

7. Which one of the following is NOT an advantage of the interview method of collecting data? It
   A. enables interviewer to judge the person interviewed on such matters as general attitude, knowledge, etc.
   B. helps build up personal relations for later installation of changes
   C. is a flexible method that can be adjusted to changing circumstances
   D. permits the obtaining of *off the record* information
   E. produces more accurate information than other methods

8. Which one of the following may be defined as a *regularly recurring appraisal of the manner in which all elements of agency management are being carried out*?
   A. Functional survey   B. Operations audit
   C. Organization survey   D. Over-all survey
   E. Reconnaissance survey

9. An analysis of the flow of work in a department should begin with the _____ work.
   A. major routine   B. minor routine   C. supervisory
   D. technical   E. unusual

10. Which method would MOST likely be used to get first-hand information on complaints from the public?
    A. Study of correspondence
    B. Study of work volume
    C. Tracing specific transactions through a series of steps
    D. Tracing use of forms
    E. Worker desk audit

11. People will generally produce the MOST if   11.____
    A. management exercises close supervision over the work
    B. there is strict discipline in the group
    C. they are happy in their work
    D. they feel involved in their work
    E. they follow *the one best way*

12. The normal analysis of which chart listed below is MOST closely related to   12.____
    organizational analysis? _____ chart.
    A. Layout   B. Operation   C. Process
    D. Work count   E. Work distribution

13. The work count would be LEAST helpful in accomplishing which one of the   13.____
    following?
    A. Demonstrating personnel needs   B. Improving the sequence of steps
    C. Measuring the value of a step   D. Spotting bottlenecks
    E. Stimulating interest in work

14. Which one of the following seems LEAST useful as a guide in interviewing   14.____
    an employee in a procedure and methods survey?
    A. Explaining who you are and the purpose of your visit
    B. Having a general plan of what you intend to get from the interview
    C. Listening carefully and not interrupting
    D. Trying out his reactions to your ideas for improvements
    E. Trying to analyze his reasons for saying what he says

15. Which one of the following is an advantage of the questionnaire method of   15.____
    gathering facts as compared with the interview method?
    A. Different people may interpret the questions differently
    B. Less *off the record* information is given
    C. More time may be taken in order to give exact answers
    D. Personal relationships with the people involved are not established
    E. There is less need for follow-up

16. Which one of the following is generally NOT an advantage of the personal   16.____
    observation method of gathering facts? It
    A. enables staff to use *off the record* information if personally observed
    B. helps in developing valid recommendations
    C. helps the person making the observation acquire *know how* valuable for
       later installation and follow-up
    D. is economical in time and money
    E. may turn up other problems in need of solution

17. Which of the following would MOST often be the best way to minimize   17.____
    resistance to change?
    A. Break the news about the change gently to the people affected
    B. Increase the salary of the people affected by the change
    C. Let the people concerned participate at the decision to change

D. Notify all people concerned with the change, both orally and in writing
E. Stress the advantages of the new system

18. The functional organization chart
    A. does not require periodic revision
    B. includes a description of the duties of each organization segment
    C. includes positions and titles for each organization segment
    D. is the simplest type of organization chart
    E. is used primarily by newly established agencies

    18.____

19. The principle of span of control has frequently been said to be in conflict with the
    A. principle of unity of command
    B. principle that authority should be commensurate with responsibility
    C. principle that like functions should be grouped into one unit
    D. principle that the number of levels between the top of an organization and the bottom should be small
    E. scalar principle

    19.____

20. If an executive delegates to his subordinates authority to handle problems of a routine nature for which standard solutions have been established, he may expect that
    A. fewer complaint will be received
    B. he has made it more difficult for his subordinates to solve these problems
    C. he has opened the way for confusion in his organization
    D. there will be a lack of consistency in the methods applied to the solution of these problems
    E. these routine problems will be handled efficiently and he will have more time for other non-routine work

    20.____

21. Which of the following would MOST likely be achieved by a change in the basic organization structure from the *process* or *functional* type to the *purpose* or *product* type?
    A. Easier recruitment of personnel in a tight labor market
    B. Fixing responsibility at a lower level in the organization
    C. Greater centralization
    D. Greater economy
    E. Greater professional development

    21.____

22. Usually the MOST difficult problem in connection with a major reorganization is
    A. adopting a pay plan to fit the new structure
    B. bringing the organization manual up-to-date
    C. determining the new organization structure
    D. gaining acceptance of the new plan by the higher level employees
    E. gaining acceptance of the new plan by the lower level employees

    22.____

23. Which of the following statements MOST accurately describes the work of the chiefs of MOST staff divisions in departments?
Chiefs
    A. focus more on getting the job done than on how it is done
    B. are mostly interested in short-range results
    C. nearly always advise but rarely advise
    D. usually command or control but rarely advise
    E. provide service to the rest of the organization and/or assist the chief executive in planning and controlling operations

23.____

24. In determining the type of organization structure of an enterprise, the one factor that might be given relatively greater weight in a small organization than in a larger organization of the same nature is the
    A. geographical location of the enterprise
    B. individual capabilities of incumbents
    C. method of financing to be employed
    D. size of the area served
    E. type of activity engaged in

24.____

25. Functional foremanship differs MOST markedly from generally accepted principle of administration in that it advocates
    A. an unlimited span of control
    B. less delegation of responsibility
    C. more than one supervisor for an employee
    D. nonfunctional organization
    E. substitution of execution for planning

25.____

KEY (CORRECT ANSWERS)

1.	A		11.	D
2.	B		12.	E
3.	A		13.	B
4.	E		14.	D
5.	A		15.	C
6.	E		16.	D
7.	E		17.	C
8.	B		18.	B
9.	A		19.	D
10.	A		20.	E

21. B
22. D
23. E
24. B
25. C

TEST 2

DIRECTIONS: Each question or incomplete statement is followed by several suggested answers or completions. Select the one that BEST answers the question or completes the statement. *PRINT THE LETTER OF THE CORRECT ANSWER IN THE SPACE AT THE RIGHT.*

1. Decentralization of the authority to make decisions is a necessary result of increased complexity in an organization, but for the sake of efficiency and coordination of operations, such decentralization must be planned carefully. A good general rule is that
    A. any decision should be made at the lowest possible point in the organization where all the information and competence necessary for a sound decision are available
    B. any decision should be made at the highest possible point in the organization, thus guaranteeing the best decision
    C. any decision should be made at the lowest possible point in the organization, but always approved by management
    D. any decision should be made by management and referred to the proper subordinate for comment
    E. no decision should be made by any individual in the organization without approval by a superior

    1.____

2. One drawback of converting a conventional consecutive filing system to a terminal digit filing system for a large installation is that
    A. conversion would be expensive in time and manpower
    B. conversion would prevent the proper use of recognized numeric classification systems, such as the Dewey decimal, in classifying files material
    C. responsibility for proper filing cannot be pinpointed in the terminal digit system
    D. the terminal digit system requires considerably more space than a normal filing system

    2.____

3. The basic filing system that would ordinarily be employed in a large administrative headquarters unit is the _____ file system.
    A   alphabetic   B. chronological
    C. mnemonic   D. retention
    E. subject classification

    3.____

4. A records center is of benefit in a records management program PRIMARILY because
    A. all the records of the organization are kept in one place
    B. inactive records can be stored economically in less expense storage areas
    C. it provides a place where useless records can be housed at little or no cost to the organization

    4.____

37

D. obsolete filing and storage equipment can be utilized out of view of the public
E. records analysts can examine an organization's files without affecting the unit's operation or upsetting the supervisors

5. In examining a number of different forms to see whether any could be combined or eliminated, which of the following would one be MOST likely to use?
   A. Forms analysis sheet of recurring data
   B. Forms control log
   C. Forms design and approval request
   D. Forms design and guide sheet
   E. Numerical file

6. The MOST important reason for control of *bootleg* forms is that
   A. they are more expensive than authorized forms
   B. they are usually poorly designed
   C. they can lead to unnecessary procedures
   D. they cannot be reordered as easily as authorized terms
   E. violation of rules and regulations should not be allowed

7. With a box design of a form, the caption title or question to be answered should be located in the _____ of the box.
   A. center at the bottom
   B. center at the top
   C. lower left corner
   D. lower right corner
   E. upper left corner

8. A two-part snapout form would be MOST properly justified if
   A. it is a cleaner operation
   B. it is prepared ten times a week
   C. it saves time in preparation
   D. it is to be filled out by hand rather than by typewriter
   E. proper registration is critical

9. When deciding whether or not to approve a request for a new form, which reference is normally MOST pertinent?
   A. Alphabetical Forms File
   B. Functional Forms File
   C. Numerical Forms File
   D. Project Completion Report
   E. Records Retention Data

10. Which of the following statements BEST explains the significance of the famed Hawthorne Plant experiments?
    They showed that
    A. a large span of control leads to more production than a small span of control
    B. morale has no relationship to production
    C. personnel counseling is of relatively little importance in a going organization

D. the special attention received by a group in an experimental situation has a greater impact on production than changes in working conditions
E. there is a direct relationship between the amount of illumination and production

11. Which of the following would most often NOT result from a highly efficient management control system?
    A. Facilitation of delegation
    B. Highlighting of problem areas
    C. Increase in willingness of people to experiment or to take calculated risks
    D. Provision of an objective test of new ideas or new methods and procedures
    E. Provision of information useful for revising objectives, programs, and operations

11._____

12. The PERT system is a
    A. method for laying out office space on a modular basis utilizing prefabricated partitions
    B. method of motivating personnel to be continuously alert and to improve their appearance
    C. method of program planning and control using a network or flow plan
    D. plan for expanding reporting techniques
    E. simplified method of cost accounting

12._____

13. The term *management control* is MOST frequently used to mean
    A. an objective and unemotional approach by management
    B. coordinating the efforts of all parts of the organization
    C. evaluation of results in relation to plan
    D. giving clear, precise orders to subordinates
    E. keeping unions from making managerial decisions

13._____

14. Which one of the following factors has the MOST bearing on the frequency with which a control report should be made?
    A. Degree of specialization of the work
    B. Degree of variability in activities
    C. Expense of the report
    D. Number of levels of supervision
    E. Number of personnel involved

14._____

15. The value of statistical records is MAINLY dependent upon the
    A. method of presenting the material
    B. number of items used
    C. range of cases sampled
    D. reliability of the information used
    E. time devoted to compiling the material

15._____

16. When a supervisor delegates an assignment, he should
    A. delegate his responsibility for the assignment
    B. make certain that the assignment is properly performed
    C. participate in the beginning and final stages of the assignment
    D. retail all authority needed to complete the assignment
    E. oversee all stages of the assignment

16.____

17. Assume that the department in which you are employed has never given official sanction to a mid-afternoon coffee break. Some bureaus have it and others do not. In the latter case, some individuals merely absent themselves for about 15 minutes at 3 P.M. while others remain on the job despite the fatigue which seems to be common among all employees in this department at that time.
    The course of action which you should recommend, if possible, is to
    A. arrange a schedule of mid-afternoon coffee breaks for all employees
    B. forbid all employees to take a mid-afternoon coffee break
    C. permit each bureau to decide for itself whether or not it will have a coffee break
    D. require all employees who wish a coffee break to take a shorter lunch period
    E. arrange a poll to discover the consensus of the department

17.____

18. The one of the following which is LEAST important in the management of a suggestion program is
    A. giving awards which are of sufficient value to encourage competition
    B. securing full support from the department's officers and executives
    C. publicizing the program and the awards given
    D. holding special conferences to analyze and evaluate some of the suggestions needed
    E. providing suggestion boxes in numerous locations

18.____

19. The one of the following which is MOST likely to decrease morale is
    A. insistence on strict adherence to safety rules
    B. making each employee responsible for the tidiness of his work area
    C. overlooking evidence of hostility between groups of employees
    D. strong, aggressive leadership
    E. allocating work on the basis of personal knowledge of the abilities and interests of the member of the department

19.____

20. Assume that a certain office procedure has been standard practice for many years.
    When a new employee asks why this particular procedure is followed, the supervisor should FIRST
    A. explain that everyone does it that way
    B. explain the reason for the procedure
    C. inform him that it has always been done that way in that particular office
    D. tell him to try it for a while before asking questions
    E. tell him he has never thought about it that way

20.____

21. Several employees complain informally to their supervisor regarding some new procedures which have been instituted.
    The supervisor should IMMEDIATELY
    A. explain that management is responsible
    B. state frankly that he had nothing to do with it
    C. refer the matter to the methods analyst
    D. tell the employees to submit their complaint as a formal grievance
    E. investigate the complaint

21.____

22. A new employee asks his supervisor how he is doing. Actually, he is not doing well in some phases of the job, but it is felt that he will learn in time.
    The BEST response for the supervisor to make is:
    A. Some things you are doing well, and in others I am sure you will improve.
    B. Wait until the end of your probation period when we will discuss this matter.
    C. You are not doing too well.
    D. You are doing very well.
    E. I'll be able to tell you when I go over your record.

22.____

23. The PRINCIPAL aim of a supervisor is to
    A. act as liaison between employee and management
    B. get the work done
    C. keep up morale
    D. train his subordinates
    E. become chief of the department

23.____

24. When the work of two bureaus must be coordinated, direct contact between the subordinates in each bureau who are working on the problem is
    A. *bad*, because it violates the chain of command
    B. *bad*, because they do not have authority to make decisions
    C. *good*, because it enable quicker results
    D. *good*, because it relieves their superiors of any responsibilities
    E. *bad*, because they may work at cross purposes

24.____

25. Of the following, the organization defect which can be ascertained MOST readily merely by analyzing an accurate and well-drawn organization chart is
    A. ineffectiveness of an activity
    B. improper span of control
    C. inappropriate assignment of functions
    D. poor supervision
    E. unlawful delegation of authority

25.____

KEY (CORRECT ANSWERS)

1.	A	11.	C
2.	A	12.	C
3.	E	13.	C
4.	B	14.	B
5.	A	15.	D
6.	C	16.	B
7.	E	17.	A
8.	E	18.	E
9.	B	19.	C
10.	D	20.	B

21.	E
22.	A
23.	B
24.	C
25.	B

EXAMINATION SECTION
TEST 1

DIRECTIONS: Each question or incomplete statement is followed by several suggested answers or completions. Select the one that BEST answers the question or completes the statement. *PRINT THE LETTER OF THE CORRECT ANSWER IN THE SPACE AT THE RIGHT.*

1. In performing a systems study, the analyst may find it necessary to prepare an accurate record of working statistics from departmental forms, questionnaires, and information gleaned in interviews.
   Which one of the following statements dealing with the statistical part of the study is the MOST valid?

   A. The emphasis of every survey is data collection.
   B. Data should not be represented in narrative form.
   C. The statistical report should include the titles of personnel required for each processing task.
   D. In gathering facts, the objective of a systems study should be the primary consideration

2. The most direct method of obtaining information about activities in the area under study is by observation. There are several general rules for an analyst that are essential for observing and being accepted as an observer.
   The one of the following statements relating to this aspect of an analyst's responsibility that is most valid in the initial phase is that the analyst should NOT

   A. limit himself to observing only; he may criticize operations and methods
   B. prepare himself for what he is about to observe
   C. obtain permission of the department's management to actually perform some of the clerical tasks himself
   D. offer views of impending charges regarding new staff requirements, equipment, or procedures

3. The active concern of the systems analyst is the study and documentation of what he observes as it exists. Before attempting the actual study and documentation, the analyst should comply with certain generally accepted procedures.
   Of the following, the step the analyst should *generally lake* FIRST is to

   A. define the problem and prepare a statement of objectives
   B. confer with the project director concerning persons to be interviewed
   C. accumulate data from all available sources within the area under study
   D. meet with operations managers to enlist their cooperation

4. During the course of any systems study, the analyst will have to gather some statistics if the operation model is to be realistic and meaningful.
   With respect to the statistical report part of the study, it is MOST valid to say that

A. it must follow a standard format since there should be no variation from one study to the next
B. the primary factor to be considered is the volume of work in the departmental unit at each stage of completion
C. only variations that occur during peak and slow periods should be recorded
D. unless deadlines in the departmental units studied by the analyst occur constantly, they should not be taken into account

5. In systems analysis, the interview is one of the analyst's major sources of information. In conducting an interview, he should strive for immediate rapport with the operations manager or department head with whom he deals.
With respect to his responsibility in this area, it is considered LEAST appropriate for the analyst to

   A. explain the full background of the study and the scope of the investigation
   B. emphasize the importance of achieving the stated objectives and review the plan of the project
   C. assume that the attitudes of the workers are less important than those of the executives
   D. request the manager's assistance in the form of questions, suggestions, and general cooperation

6. Large, complex endeavors often take a long time to implement. The following statements relate to long lead times imposed by large-scale endeavors.
Select the one usually considered to be LEAST valid.

   A. Where there are external sponsors who provide funds or political support, they should be provided with some demonstration of what is being accomplished.
   B. Long lead times simplify planning and diminish the threat of obsolescence by assuring that objectives will be updated by the time the project is nearing completion.
   C. During the period when no tangible results are forthcoming, techniques must be found to assess progress.
   D. Employees, particularly scientific personnel, should feel a sense of accomplishment or they may shy away from research which involves long-term commitments.

7. In traditional management theory, administrators are expected to collect and weigh facts and probabilities, make an optimal decision and see that it is carried out.
In the management of large-scale development projects, such a clear sequence of action is *generally* NOT possible because of

   A. their limited duration
   B. the static and fixed balance of power among interest groups
   C. continuous suppression of new facts
   D. constantly changing constraints and pressures

Questions 8-10.

DIRECTIONS: One of the most valuable parts of the systems package is the systems flowchart, a technique that aids understanding of the work flow. A flowchart should depict all the intricacies of the work flow from start to finish in order to give the onlooker a solid picture at a glance. The table below contains symbols used by the analyst in flowcharting. In answering Questions 8 through 10, refer to the following figures.

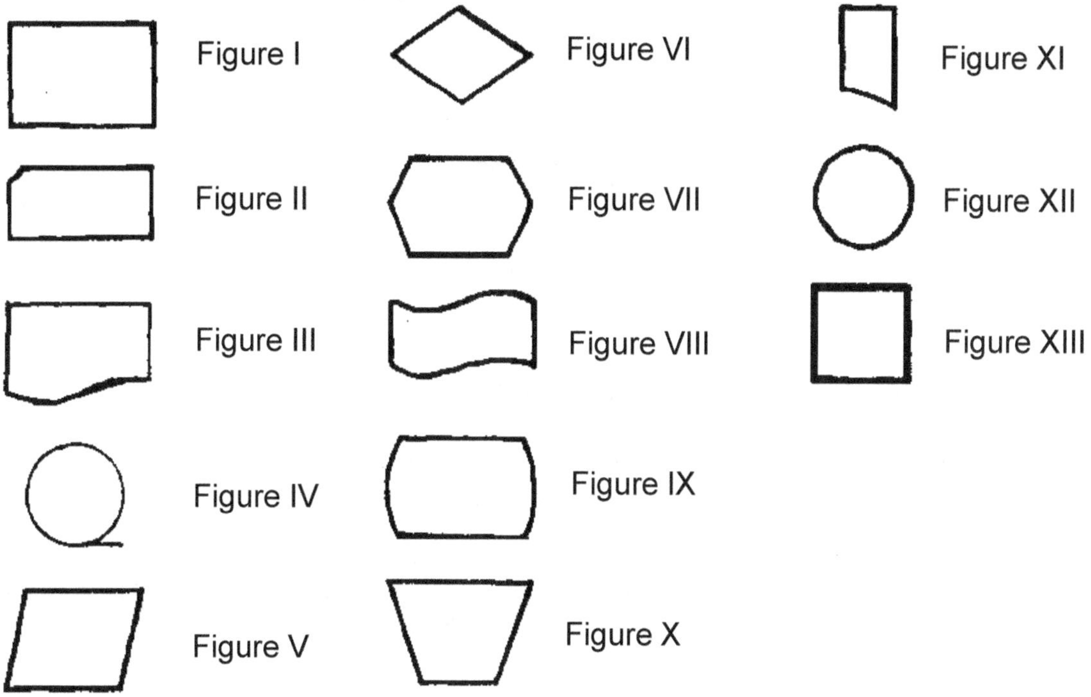

Figure I
Figure II
Figure III
Figure IV
Figure V
Figure VI
Figure VII
Figure VIII
Figure IX
Figure X
Figure XI
Figure XII
Figure XIII

8. The symbol that is COMMONLY used to specify clerical procedures which are not essential to the main processing function and yet are part of the overall procedure is represented by Figure

   A. III   B. VI   C. XII   D. XIII

9. An analyst wishes to designate the following activities:
   File reports; Calculate average; Attach labels.
   The MOST APPROPRIATE symbol to use is represented by Figure

   A. V   B. VI   C. VII   D. II

10. A *Report, Journal,* or *Record* should be represented by Figure

    A. I   B. III   C. IX   D. XI

Question 11.

DIRECTIONS: The following figures are often used in program and systems flowcharting.

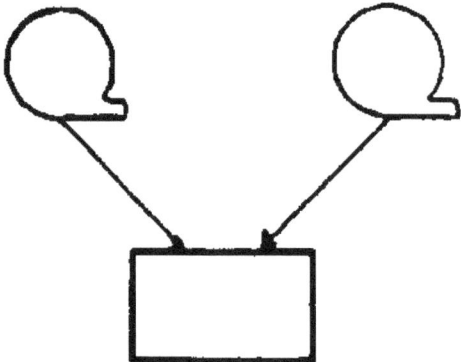

11. The above figures represent

    A. two storage discs incorporated in a processing function
    B. two report papers to be put in a cabinet in chronological order
    C. two transmittal tapes—both externally generated—routed to a vault
    D. an auxiliary operation involving two sequential decisions

12. When research and analysis of government programs, e.g., pest control, drug rehabilitation, etc., is sponsored and conducted within a government unit, the scope of the analysis should *generally* be _____ the scope of the authority of the manager to whom the analyst is responsible.

    A. less than
    B. less than or equal to
    C. greater than or equal to
    D. greater than

13. In recent years, there has been an increasing emphasis on outputs—the goods and services that a program produces. This emphasis on outputs imposes an information requirement. The one of the following which would MOST likely NOT be considered output information in a hospital or health care program is the

    A. number of patients cared for
    B. number of days patients were hospitalized
    C. budgeted monies for hospital beds
    D. quality of the service

14. Which one of the following statements pertaining to management information systems is generally considered to be LEAST valid?

    A. A management information system is a network of related subsystems developed according to an integrated scheme for evaluating the activities of an agency.
    B. A management information system specifies the content and format, the preparation and integration of information for all various functions within an agency that will best satisfy needs at various levels of management.
    C. To operate a successful management information system, an agency will require a complex electronic computer installation.
    D. The five elements which compose a management information system are: data input, files, data processing, procedures, and data output.

15. In the field of records management, electronic equipment is being used to handle office paperwork or data processing. With respect to such use, of the following, it is MOST valid to say that

    A. electronic equipment is not making great strides in the achievement of speed and economy in office paperwork
    B. electronic equipment accelerates the rate at which office paperwork is completed
    C. paperwork problems can be completely solved through mechanization
    D. introduction of electronic data processing equipment cuts down on the paper consumed in office processes

16. A reports control program evaluates the reporting requirements of top management so that reviews can be made of the existing reporting system to determine its adequacy. Of the following statements pertaining to reports control, which is the MOST likely to be characteristic of such a program?

    A. Only the exception will be reported
    B. Preparation of daily reports will be promoted
    C. Executives will not delegate responsibility for preparing reports
    D. Normal conditions are reported

17. Which of the following types of work measurement techniques requires the HIGHEST degree of training and skill of technicians and supervisors and is MOST likely to involve the HIGHEST original cost?

    A. Work sampling
    B. Predetermined time standards
    C. The time study (stopwatch timing)
    D. Employee reporting

18. Which of the following types of work measurement techniques *generally* requires the LEAST amount of time to measure and establish standards?

    A. Work sampling
    B. Predetermined time standards
    C. The time study (stopwatch timing)
    D. Employee reporting

19. Assume that you, as an analyst, have been assigned to formally organize small work groups within a city department to perform a special project. After studying the project, you find you must choose between two possible approaches—either task teams or highly functionalized groups.
    What would be one of the advantages of choosing the task-team approach over the highly functionalized organization?

    A. Detailed, centralized planning would be encouraged.
    B. Indifference to city goals and restrictions on output would be lessened.
    C. Work would be divided into very specialized areas.
    D. Superiors would be primarily concerned with seeing that subordinates do not deviate from the project.

20. In systems theory, there is a *what-if* method of treating uncertainty that explores the effect on the alternatives of environmental change. This method is generally referred to as _____ analysis.

   A. sensitivity
   B. contingency
   C. a fortiori
   D. systems

KEY (CORRECT ANSWERS)

1. D
2. D
3. A
4. B
5. C
6. B
7. D
8. D
9. A
10. B
11. A
12. B
13. C
14. C
15. B
16. A
17. B
18. A
19. B
20. B

TEST 2

DIRECTIONS: Each question or incomplete statement is followed by several suggested answers or completions. Select the one that BEST answers the question or completes the statement. *PRINT THE LETTER OF THE CORRECT ANSWER IN THE SPACE AT THE RIGHT.*

1. Which of the following systems exists at the strategic level of an organization?

    A. Decision support system (DSS)
    B. Executive support system (ESS)
    C. Knowledge work system (KWS)
    D. Management information system (MIS)

2. The functions of knowledge workers in an organization generally include each of the following EXCEPT

    A. updating knowledge
    B. managing documentation of knowledge
    C. serving as internal consultants
    D. acting as change agents

3. Which of the following is not a management benefit associated with end-user development of information systems?

    A. Reduced application backlog
    B. Increased user satisfaction
    C. Simplified testing and documentation procedures
    D. Improved requirements determination

4. Assume that an analyst is preparing an analysis of a departmental program. His investigation leads him to a potential problem relating to the program. The analyst thinks the potential problem is so serious that he cannot rely on preventive actions to remove the cause or significantly reduce the probability of its occurrence.
Of the following, the MOST appropriate way for the analyst to promptly handle this serious matter described above would be to

    A. apply systematic afterthought to the achievement of objectives by analysis of the problem
    B. compare actual performance with the expected standard of performance
    C. prepare contingency actions to be adopted immediately if the problem does occur
    D. identify, locate, and describe the deviation from the standard

5. Assume that an analyst is directed to investigate a problem relating to organizational behavior in his agency and to prepare a report thereon. After reviewing the preliminary draft, his superior cautions him to overcome his tendency to misuse and overgeneralize his interpretation of existing knowledge.
Which one of the following statements appearing in the draft is MOST *usually* considered to be a common distortion of behavioral science knowledge?

    A. Pay—even incentive pay—isn't very important anymore.
    B. There are nonrational aspects to people's behavior.
    C. The informal system exerts much control over organizational participants.
    D. Employees have many motives.

Questions 6-10.

DIRECTIONS: Each of Questions 6 through 10 consists of a statement which contains one word that is incorrectly used because it is not in keeping with the meaning that the quotation is evidently intended to convey. Determine which word is incorrectly used. Then select from the words lettered A, B, C, or D the word which, when substituted for the incorrectly used word, would BEST help to convey the meaning of the statement.

6. While the utilization of cost-benefit analysis in decision-making processes should be encouraged, it must be well understood that there are many limitations on the constraints of the analysis. One must be cautioned against using cost-benefit procedures automatically and blindly. Still, society will almost certainly be better off with the application of cost-benefit methods than it would be without them. As some authorities aptly point out, an important advantage of a cost-benefit study is that it forces those responsible to quantify costs and benefits as far as possible rather than rest content with vague qualitative judgments or personal hunches. Also, such an analysis has the very valuable byproduct of causing questions to be asked which would otherwise not have been raised. Finally, even if cost-benefit analysis cannot give the right answer, it can sometimes play the purely negative role of screening projects and rejecting those answers which are obviously less promising.

   A. precise
   B. externally
   C. applicability
   D. unresponsiveness

7. The programming method used by the government should attempt to assess the costs and benefits of individual projects, in comparison with private and other public alternatives. The program, then, consists of the most meritorious projects that the budget will design. Meritorious projects excluded from the budget provide arguments for increasing its size. There are difficulties inherent in the specific project approach. The attempt is to apply profit criteria in public projects analogous to those used in evaluating private projects. This involves comparison of monetary values of present and future costs and benefits. But, in many important cases, such as highways, parkways, and bridges, the product of the government's investment does not directly enter the market economy. Consequently, evaluation requires imputation of market values. For example, the returns on a bridge have been estimated by attempting to value the time saved by users. Such measurements necessarily contain a strong, element of artificiality.

   A. annulled   B. expedient   C. accommodate   D. marginally

8. Consider the problem of budgeting for activities designed to alleviate poverty and rooted unemployment. Are skill retraining efforts better or worse investments than public works? Are they better or worse than subsidies or other special incentives to attract new industry? Or, at an even more fundamental level, is a dollar invested in an attempt to rehabilitate a mature, technologically displaced, educationally handicapped, unemployed man a better commitment than a comparable dollar invested in supporting the educational and technical preparation of his son for employment in a different line of work? The questions may look unreasonable, even unanswerable. But the fact is that they are implicitly answered in any budget decision in the defined problem area. The only subordinate issue is whether the answer rests on intuition and guess, or on a budget system that presents relevant information so organized as to contribute to rational analysis, planning, and decision-making.

   A. incomplete
   B. relevant
   C. significant
   D. speculate

9. Choices among health programs, on the basis of cost-benefit analysis, raise another set of ethical problems. Measuring discounted lifetime earnings does not reveal the value of alleviating pain and suffering; some diseases have a high death rate, others are debilitating, others are merely uncomfortable. In general, choices among health and education programs that are predicated on discounted lifetime earnings will structure the choice against those who have low earnings, those whose earnings will materialize only at some future point in time, or those whose participation in the labor force is limited. It may be an appropriate economic policy to reduce expenditures in areas that maximize the future level of national income. But the maximization of social welfare may dictate attention to considerations, such as equality of opportunity, that transcend the limitations of values defined in such narrow terms.

    A. concentrate   B. divergent   C. enforcing   D. favorably

10. Without defined and time-phased objectives, it is difficult to be critical of administrative performance. To level a charge of waste or malperformance at the managers of a public program is, of course, one of the more popular pastimes of any administration's loyal opposition. But it is a rare experience to find such a charge documented by the kind of precise cost-effectiveness measures that are the common test of the quality of management performance in a well-run organization. Those who take a professional view of management responsibility are even more concerned about the acceptance of the kind of information that would enable a manager to assess the progress and quality of his own performance and, as appropriate, to initiate corrective action before outside criticism can even start.

    A. absence   B. rebut   C. withdraw   D. impeded

11. What is the relationship between the cost of inputs and the value of outputs when the results obtained from a program can be measured in money? _____ ratio.

    A. Value administrative-cost
    B. Break-even point
    C. Variable-direct
    D. Cost-benefit

12. Some writers in the field of public expenditure have noted a disturbing tendency inherent in cost-benefit analysis. Which one of the following statements MOST accurately expresses their concern over the use of cost-benefit analysis? It

    A. encourages the attachment of monetary values to intangibles
    B. has a built-in neglect of measurable outcomes while emphasizing the nonmeasurable
    C. consciously exaggerates social values and overstates political values
    D. encourages emphasis of those costs and benefits that cannot be measured rather than those that can

13. In private industry, budgetary control begins logically with an estimate of sales and the income therefrom.
    Of the following, the term used in government which is MOST analogous to that of sales in private industry is

    A. borrowed funds
    B. the amount appropriated
    C. general overhead
    D. surplus funds

14. When constructing graphs of causally related variables, how should the variables be placed to conform to conventional use?

    A. The independent variable should be placed on the vertical axis and the dependent variable on the horizontal axis.
    B. The dependent variable should be placed on the vertical axis and the independent variable on the horizontal axis.
    C. Independent variables should be placed on both axes.
    D. Dependent variables should be placed on both axes.

Questions 15-18.

DIRECTIONS: Answer Questions 15 through 18 on the basis of the following graph describing the output of computer operators.

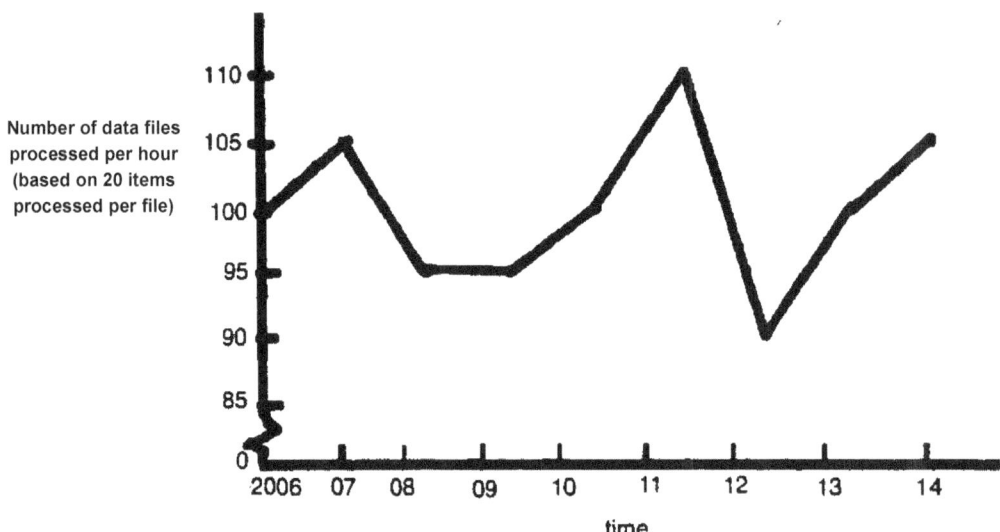

15. Of the following, during what four-year period did the AVERAGE OUTPUT of computer operators *fall below* 100 data files per hour?

    A. 2007-10   B. 2008-11   C. 2010-13   D. 2011-14

16. The AVERAGE PERCENTAGE CHANGE in output over the previous year's output for the years 2009 to 2012 is MOST NEARLY

    A. 2   B. 0   C. -5   D. -7

17. The DIFFERENCE between the actual output for 2012 and the projected figure based upon the average increase from 2006 to 2011 is MOST NEARLY

    A. 18   B. 20   C. 22   D. 24

18. Assume that after constructing the above graph, you, an analyst, discovered that the average number of items processed per file in 2012 was 25 (instead of 20) because of the complex nature of the work performed during that period.
    The AVERAGE OUTPUT in files per hour for the period 2010 to 2013, expressed in terms of 20 items per file, would then be APPROXIMATELY

    A. 95   B. 100   C. 105   D. 110

19. Assume that Unit S's production fluctuated substantially from one year to another. In 2009, Unit S's production was 100% greater than in 2008; in 2010, it was 25% less than in 2009; and in 2011, it was 10% greater than in 2010. On the basis of this information, it is CORRECT to conclude that Unit S's production in 2011 exceeded its production in 2008 by

    A. 50%   B. 65%   C. 75%   D. 90%

20. Statistical sampling is often used in administrative operations primarily because it enables

    A. administrators to make staff selections
    B. decisions to be made based on mathematical and scientific fact
    C. courses of action to be determined by electronic data processing or computer programs
    D. useful predictions to be made from relatively small samples

KEY (CORRECT ANSWERS)

1. B
2. B
3. C
4. C
5. A

6. C
7. C
8. C
9. A
10. A

11. D
12. A
13. B
14. B
15. A

16. B
17. C
18. C
19. B
20. D

EXAMINATION SECTION
TEST 1

DIRECTIONS: Each question or incomplete statement is followed by several suggested answers or completions. Select the one that BEST answers the question or completes the statement. *PRINT THE LETTER OF THE CORRECT ANSWER IN THE SPACE AT THE RIGHT.*

1. In organizational theory, the optimum span of control, that is, the number of subordinates who can be effectively supervised by one man above the level of the first line supervisor is GENERALLY set at between
   A. 3 and 6   B. 6 and 12   C. 12 and 18   D. 18 and 24

   1.____

2. Which of the following is LEAST desirable as a basic guide to normal conventional office layout?
   A. Arrange desks so that work flows in a normal fashion
   B. Place files nearest to the persons who will use them
   C. Utilize a number of small areas to provide privacy
   D. Utilize one single large area

   2.____

3. *A set of objects together with relationships between the objects and between their attributes* is the definition of
   A. a perceptual whole and its subcomponents
   B. a system in the terms of specific systems theory
   C. an organism
   D. forms control

   3.____

4. A technique of time study in which each employee maintains a record of his own time is GENERALLY known as _____ study.
   A. estimated time   B. observed time
   C. time log   D. wristwatch

   4.____

5. An employee has approached a supervisor with a request for a change involving his personal status or with a suggestion for making an improvement in the work The supervisor knows that the suggestion cannot be granted.
   Of the following, the BEST procedure would be for the supervisor to
   A. refer the matter to the personnel department
   B. refer the matter to his superior for action
   C. reject the proposal, explaining the defects or objections which cannot be overcome
   D. shelve the idea so that the employee will realize it cannot be acted upon

   5.____

6. There are, in general, a number of common methods of drawing samples for statistical work.
   The method in which a regularly ordered interval is maintained between the items chosen is BEST termed _____ sampling.
   A. random   B. stratified or selective
   C. systematic   D. work

   6.____

7. The multi-column process chart can be put to all of the following general uses EXCEPT to
   A. improve office layout
   B. improve procedures
   C. standardize procedures
   D. train personnel

8. If one wished to show the percentage of change over a period of time, the MOST appropriate type of graph or chart GENERALLY would be the _____ chart.
   A. bar
   B. line or curve
   C. logarithmic or semilogarithmic
   D. pie

9. A chart designed for the explicit purpose of portraying graphically information relating to the degree of responsibility of key individuals for the performance of various functions is BEST described as a(n) _____ chart.
   A. linear responsibility
   B. work distribution
   C. work process
   D. staff

10. The technique of work measurement LEAST useful for setting up a program of office incentive pay GENERALLY would be
    A. log sheets
    B. stopwatch time study
    C. wristwatch time study
    D. work sampling

11. There are a number of steps to be taken in making a work sampling study in order to set production standards. Three of the steps listed below are peculiar only to work sampling, in contrast with other work measurement techniques.
    The one EXCEPTION is:
    A. Define the breakdown of work into the proper elements of work and no-work or delay to be observed
    B. Determine the required number of observations needed for the specified degree of reliability
    C. Establish the observation intervals
    D. Make a preliminary estimate of work and no-work or delay element percentages for step A

12. A number of standardized flow process chart symbols have been generally accepted.
    The symbol v̄ GENERALLY indicates a(n)
    A. delay
    B. storage or file
    C. inspection
    D. operation

13. The number of standardized flow process chart symbols have been generally accepted.
    The symbol ▭ GENERALLY indicates a(n)
    A. delay
    B. storage or file
    C. inspection
    D. operation

14. The type of work for which short interval scheduling generally would be LEAST applicable would be the work of a group of
    A. calculating clerks
    B. order clerks
    C. technically-oriented clerks
    D. typists

15. In writing a business report, the BEST expression to use, in general, of those listed below would NORMALLY be:
    A. Because
    B. Inasmuch as
    C. In view of the fact that
    D. With reference to

16. Of the following, the MAJOR advantage of a random access data processing system, as compared with a sequential-type system, is its
    A. ability to use more than one input system
    B. demand for more sophisticated systems and programming
    C. greater storage capacity and access speed
    D. potential for processing data on a *first come, first-served* basis

17. A good rule to remember with regard to decision making is that decisions should be made
    A. at the highest level competent to make such a decision
    B. at the lowest level competent to make such a decision
    C. by the person responsible for carrying out the decision
    D. by the person responsible for the work of the unit

18. Which of the following potential systems would LEAST likely be improved by being online? A(n) _____ system.
    A. budgeting control
    B. welfare eligibility
    C. employee payroll
    D. inventory control

19. A management information and control system essentially should be designed to provide management personnel with up-to-date information which will enable them to improve control over their operations.
    In designing such a system, the FIRST step to determine is:
    A. What information is needed to effectively control operations?
    B. What information is presently available?
    C. What organization changes are necessary to implement the system?
    D. Who is presently processing the information that might be used?

20. In designing control reports, which of the following guidelines is of MOST importance?
    A. Financial information should always be carried to the nearest penny.
    B. The report should be a simple and concise statement of only the pertinent facts.
    C. The report should indicate the source of original data and how the computations were made.
    D. The report should have the broadest possible distribution at all levels of management.

21. A situation which enables a number of users at offsite locations to have access to an office computer network is called
    A. multiprocessing
    B. multiprogramming
    C. cloud connectivity
    D. remote access

22. Computer software that would typically be used for widespread dissemination of a business report is
    A. Microsoft Word
    B. Microsoft PowerPoint
    C. Adobe Elements
    D. Google Sheets

23. Which of the following steps is LEAST desirable in designing an electronic data processing system?
    A. Design the EDP system first, then relate it to current operations
    B. Develop a corollary chart for the corresponding flow of information
    C. Develop a flow chart for the functions affected by the system
    D. Obtain from available EDP equipment that which best fits current operations

24. Electronic data processing equipment can produce more information faster than can be generated by any other means. Because this is true, one wonders whether our ability to generate information has not far outstripped our ability to assimilate it.
    In view of this, a PERSISTENT danger management faces is in
    A. determining the budget for management information systems
    B. determining what information is of real worth
    C. finding enough computer personnel
    D. keeping their computers fully occupied

25. The one of the following that is an ADVANTAGE of a hybrid local/remote network setup over fully local access is
    A. the ability to access a network outside normal circumstances
    B. closer oversight of personnel
    C. more efficient workflow
    D. reduced costs for software and production equipment

KEY (CORRECT ANSWERS)

1.	A	11.	A
2.	C	12.	B
3.	A	13.	C
4.	C	14.	C
5.	C	15.	A
6.	C	16.	D
7.	A	17.	B
8.	C	18.	C
9.	A	19.	A
10.	A	20.	B

21.	D
22.	A
23.	A
24.	B
25.	A

TEST 2

DIRECTIONS: Each question or incomplete statement is followed by several suggested answers or completions. Select the one that BEST answers the question or completes the statement. *PRINT THE LETTER OF THE CORRECT ANSWER IN THE SPACE AT THE RIGHT.*

1. In analyzing data for the acquisition of new equipment, an analyst gathers the facts, analyzes them, and develops new procedures which will be required when the new equipment arrives.
Inn analyzing the factors involved, which one of the following is normally LEAST important in the evaluation of new equipment?
    A. Cost factors
    B. Layout and installation factors
    C. Production planning
    D. Operational experience of manufacturers of allied equipment

1._____

2. If an analyst is required to recommend the selection of a machine for an office operation, he can BEST judge the expected output of a particular machine by pursuing which of the following courses of action?
Obtain
    A. an actual test run of the machine in his office
    B. data from the manufacturer of the machine
    C. information on the percentage of working time the machine will be used
    D. the experience of actual users of similar machines elsewhere

2._____

3. Of the following, the BEST definition of records management is
    A. storage of all types of records at minimum expense
    B. planned control of all types of records
    C. storage of records for maximum accessibility
    D. systematic filing of all types of records

3._____

4. The one of the following which is NOT a primary objective of a records retention and disposal system is to
    A. assure appropriate preservation of records having permanent value
    B. dispose of records not warranting further preservation
    C. establish retention standards for archives
    D. provide an opportunity to use miniaturization

4._____

5. Of the following functions of management, the one which should NORMALLY precede the others is
    A. coordinating   B. directing   C. organizing   D. planning

5._____

6. One of the more famous studies of organizations is called the Hawthorne study.
This work was one of the first to point out the importance of
    A. employee's benefit and retirement programs
    B. informal organization among employees
    C. job engineering
    D. styles of position classification

6._____

7. In organization theory, the type of position in which an individual is appointed to give technical aid to management on a particular problem area is generally BEST termed a(n)
   A. administrative assistant
   B. assistant to
   C. staff assistant
   D. staff specialist

8. In organizing, doing what works in the particular situation, with due regard to both short- and long-range objective, is BEST termed
   A. ambivalence
   B. authoritarianism
   C. decentralization
   D. pragmatism

9. If an effort were made to reduce the number of private offices in a new layout, the LEAST effective substitute in offering privacy would be the use of
   A. an open area with lower movable partitions or railings separating each individual
   B. conference rooms
   C. larger desks
   D. modular desk units

10. The term *administrative substation* NORMALLY refers to
    A. a work station handling a number of office services for an office organization
    B. a work station where middle level supervisors are located
    C. an office for handling management trainees
    D. the functions allocated to particular levels of administrative managers

11. An operations research technique which would be applied to determine the optimum number of window clerks or interviewers to have in an agency serving the public would MOST likely be the use of
    A. line of balance
    B. queuing theory
    C. simulation
    D. work sampling

12. A type of file which permits the operator to remain seated while the file can be moved backward and forward as required is BEST termed a _____ file.
    A. lateral
    B. movable
    C. reciprocating
    D. rotary

13. The technique of work measurement in which the analyst observes the work at random times of the day is BEST termed
    A. indirect observation
    B. logging
    C. ratio delay
    D. wristwatch

14. Examples of predetermined time systems generally should include all of the following EXCEPT
    A. Master Clerical Data
    B. Methods Time Measurement
    C. Short Interval Data
    D. Work Factor

15. A technique by which the supervisor or an assistant distributes a predetermined batch of work to the employee at periodic intervals of the day is generally BEST known as
    A. backlog control scheduling
    B. production control scheduling
    C. short interval schedule
    D. workload balancing

    15.____

16. E. Wright Bakke defined his *fusion process* as: The
    A. work environment to some degree remakes the organization and the organization to some degree remakes the work environment
    B. fusing of the interests of both management and labor unions
    C. community of interest between first line supervisors and top management
    D. organization to some degree remakes the individual and the individual to some degree remakes the organization

    16.____

17. A pamphlet on issues related to 2020s-era office setup would likely be titled
    A. Close Encounters: How Proximity Elevates Production
    B. How Connectivity Spurs Inspiration
    C. See Your Employees in a New Light With Open Floor Plans
    D. From A to Zoom: The Terminology of the Hybrid Workplace

    17.____

18. In planning office space for a newly established bureau, it would usually be LEAST desirable to
    A. concentrate, rather than disperse, the chief sources of office noises
    B. design an office environment with the same brightness as the office desk
    C. designate as reception rooms, washrooms, and other service areas those areas that will receive lesser amounts of illumination than those areas in which private office work will be performed
    D. eliminate natural light in cases where it is not the major light source

    18.____

19. A private office should be used when its use is dictated by facts and unbiased judgment. It should never be provided simply because requests and sometimes pressure have been brought to bear.
    Of the following reasons used to justify use of a private office, the one that requires the MOST care in determining whether a private office is actually warranted is
    A. an office has always been provided for a particular job
    B. prestige considerations
    C. the confidential nature of the work
    D. the work involves high concentration

    19.____

20. Theoretically, an ideal organization structure can be set up for each enterprise. In actual practice, the ideal organization structure is seldom, if ever, obtained. Of the following, the one that normally is of LEAST influence in determining the organization structure is the
    A. existence of agreements and favors among members of the organization
    B. funds available
    C. opinions and beliefs of top executives
    D. tendency of management to discard established forms in favor of new forms

    20.____

21. An IMPORTANT aspect to keep in mind during the decision-making process is that
    A. all possible alternatives for attaining goals should be sought out and considered
    B. considering various alternatives only leads to confusion
    C. once a decision has been made, it cannot be retracted
    D. there is only one correct method to reach any goal

22. Implementation of accountability requires
    A. a leader who will not hesitate to take punitive action
    B. an established system of communication from the bottom to the top
    C. explicit directives from leaders
    D. too much expense to justify it

23. Of the following, the MAJOR difference between systems and procedures analysis and work simplification is:
    A. The former complicates organizational routine and the latter simplifies it
    B. The former is objective and the latter is subjective
    C. The former generally utilizes expert advice and the latter is a *do-it-yourself* improvement by supervisors and workers
    D. There is no difference other than in name

24. Systems development is concerned with providing
    A. a specific set of work procedures
    B. an overall framework to describe general relationships
    C. definitions of particular organizational functions
    D. organizational symbolism

25. Organizational systems and procedures should be
    A. developed as problems arise as no design can anticipate adequately the requirements of an organization
    B. developed jointly by experts in systems and procedures and the people who are responsible for implementing them
    C. developed solely by experts in systems and procedures
    D. eliminated whenever possible to save unnecessary expense

KEY (CORRECT ANSWERS)

1.	D	11.	B
2.	A	12.	C
3.	B	13.	C
4.	D	14.	C
5.	D	15.	C
6.	B	16.	D
7.	D	17.	D
8.	D	18.	D
9.	C	19.	A
10.	A	20.	D

21. A
22. B
23. C
24. B
25. B

TEST 3

DIRECTIONS: Each question or incomplete statement is followed by several suggested answers or completions. Select the one that BEST answers the question or completes the statement. *PRINT THE LETTER OF THE CORRECT ANSWER IN THE SPACE AT THE RIGHT.*

1. The CHIEF danger of a decentralized control system is that
   A. excessive reports and communications will be generated
   B. problem areas may not be detected readily
   C. the expense will become routine
   D. this will result in too many *chiefs*

2. Of the following, management guides and controls clerical work PRINCIPALLY through
   A. close supervision and constant checking of personnel
   B. spot checking of clerical procedures
   C. strong sanctions for clerical supervisors
   D. the use of printed forms

3. Which of the following is MOST important before conducting fact-finding interviews?
   A. Becoming acquainted with all personnel to be interviewed
   B. Explaining the techniques you plan to use
   C. Explaining to the operating officials the purpose and scope of the study
   D. Orientation of the physical layout

4. Of the following, the one that is NOT essential in carrying out a comprehensive work improvement program is
   A. standards of performance
   B. supervisory training
   C. work count/task list
   D. work distribution chart

5. Which of the following control techniques is MOST useful on large complex systems projects?
   A. A general work plan
   B. Gantt chart
   C. Monthly progress report
   D. PERT chart

6. The action which is MOST effective in gaining acceptance of a study by the agency which is being studied is
   A. a directive from the agency head to install a study based on recommendations included in a report
   B. a lecture-type presentation following approval of the procedures
   C. a written procedure in narrative form covering the proposed system with visual presentations and discussions
   D. procedural charts showing the *before* situation, forms, steps, etc. to the employees affected

7. Which of the following is NOT an advantage in the use of oral instructions as compared with written instructions? Oral instruction(s)
   A. can easily be changed
   B. is superior in transmitting complex directives
   C. facilitate exchange of information between a superior and his subordinate
   D. with discussions make it easier to ascertain understanding

8. Which organization principle is MOST closely related to procedural analysis and improvement?
   A. Duplication, overlapping, and conflict should be eliminated.
   B. Managerial authority should be clearly defined.
   C. The objectives of the organization should be clearly defined.
   D. Top management should be freed of burdensome detail.

9. Which one of the following is the MAJOR objective of operational audits?
   A. Detecting fraud
   B. Determining organization problems
   C. Determining the number of personnel needed
   D. Recommending opportunities for improving operating and management practices

10. Of the following, the formalization of organization structure is BEST achieved by
    A. a narrative description of the plan of organization
    B. functional charts
    C. job descriptions together with organization charts
    D. multi-flow charts

11. Budget planning is MOST useful when it achieves
    A. cost control
    B. forecast of receipts
    C. performance review
    D. personnel reduction

12. The UNDERLYING principle of sound administration is to
    A. base administration on investigation facts
    B. have plenty of resources available
    C. hire a strong administrator
    D. establish a broad policy

13. Although questionnaires are not the best survey tool the management analyst has to use, there are times when a good questionnaire can expedite the *fact-finding* phase of a management survey.
    Which of the following should be AVOIDED in the design and distribution of the questionnaire?
    A. Questions should be framed so that answers can be classified and tabulated for analysis.
    B. Those receiving the questionnaire must be knowledgeable enough to accurately provide the information desired.

C. The questionnaire should enable the respondent to answer in a narrative manner.
D. The questionnaire should require a minimum amount of writing.

14. Of the following, the formula which is used to calculate the arithmetic mean from data grouped in a frequency distribution is M =

    A. $\dfrac{N}{\Sigma fx}$
    B. $N(\Sigma fx)$
    C. $\dfrac{\Sigma fx}{N}$
    D. $\dfrac{\Sigma x}{fN}$

    14.____

15. Arranging large groups of numbers in frequency distributions
    A. gives a more composite picture of the total group than a random listing
    B. is misleading in most cases
    C. is unnecessary in most instances
    D. presents the data in a form whereby further manipulation of the group is eliminated

    15.____

16. After a budget has been developed, it serves to
    A. assist the accounting department in posting expenditures
    B. measure the effectiveness of department managers
    C. provide a yardstick against which actual costs are measured
    D. provide the operating department with total expenditure to date

    16.____

17. Of the following, which formula is used to determine staffing requirements?

    A. $\dfrac{\text{Hours per man-day}}{\text{Volume x Standard}}$ = Employees Needed

    B. $\dfrac{\text{Hours per man-day x Standard}}{\text{Volume}}$ = Employees Needed

    C. $\dfrac{\text{Hours per man-day x Volume}}{\text{Standard}}$ = Employees Needed

    D. $\dfrac{\text{Volume x Standard}}{\text{Hours per man-day}}$ = Employees Needed

    17.____

18. Of the following, which formula is used to determine the number of days required to process work?

    A. $\dfrac{\text{Employees x Daily Output}}{\text{Volume}}$ = Days to Process Work

    B. $\dfrac{\text{Employees x Volume}}{\text{Daily Output}}$ = Days to Process Work

    C. $\dfrac{\text{Volume}}{\text{Employees x Daily Output}}$ = Days to Process Work

    D. $\dfrac{\text{Volume x Daily Output}}{\text{Employees}}$ = Days to Process Work

    18.____

19. Identify this symbol, as used in a Systems Flow Chart.
    A. Document
    B. Decision
    C. Preparation
    D. Process

19.____

20. Of the following, the MAIN advantage of a form letter over a dictated letter is that a form letter
    A. is more expressive
    B. is neater
    C. may be mailed in a window envelope
    D. requires less secretarial time

20.____

21. The term that may be defined as a *systematic analysis of all factors affecting work being done or all factors that will affect work to be done, in order to save effort, time, or money* is
    A. flow process charting   B. work flow analysis
    C. work measurement   D. work simplification

21.____

22. Generally, the LEAST important basic factor to be considered in developing office layout improvements is to locate
    A. office equipment, reference facilities, and files as close as practicable to those using them
    B. persons as close as practicable to the persons from whom they receive their work
    C. persons as close as practicable to windows and/or adequate ventilation
    D. persons who are friendly with each other close together to improve morale

22.____

23. Of the following, the one which is LEAST effective in reducing administrative costs is
    A. applying objective measurement techniques to determine the time required to perform a given task
    B. establishing budgets on the basis of historical performance data
    C. motivating supervisors and managers in the importance of cost reduction
    D. selecting the best method—manual, mechanical, or electronic—to process the essential work

23.____

24. *Fire-fighting* is a common expression in management terminology.
    Of the following, which BEST describes *fire-fighting* as an analyst's approach to solving paperwork problems?
    A. A complete review of all phases of the department's processing functions
    B. A studied determination of the proper equipment to process the work
    C. An analysis of each form that is being processed and the logical reasons for its processing
    D. The solution of problems as they arise, usually at the request of operating personnel

24.____

25. Assume that an analyst with a proven record of accomplishment on many projects is having difficulties on his present assignment.
Of the following, the BEST course of action for his superior to take is to
   A. assume there is a personality conflict involved and transfer the analyst to another project
   B. give the analyst some time off
   C. review the nature of the project to determine whether or not the analyst is equipped to handle the assignment
   D. suggest that the analyst seek counseling

KEY (CORRECT ANSWERS)

1. B
2. D
3. C
4. B
5. D

6. C
7. B
8. A
9. D
10. C

11. A
12. A
13. C
14. C
15. A

16. C
17. D
18. C
19. A
20. D

21. D
22. D
23. B
24. D
25. C

EXAMINATION SECTION
TEST 1

DIRECTIONS: Each question or incomplete statement is followed by several suggested answers or completions. Select the one that BEST answers the question or completes the statement. *PRINT THE LETTER OF THE CORRECT ANSWER IN THE SPACE AT THE RIGHT.*

1. The MOST important factor in establishing a disciplinary policy in an organization is   1.____

    A. consistency of application
    B. strict supervisors
    C. strong enforcement
    D. the degree of toughness or laxity

2. The FIRST step in planning a program is to   2.____

    A. clearly define the objectives
    B. estimate the costs
    C. hire a program director
    D. solicit funds

3. The PRIMARY purpose of control in an organization is to   3.____

    A. punish those who do not do their job well
    B. get people to do what is necessary to achieve an objective
    C. develop clearly stated rules and regulations
    D. regulate expenditures

4. After a procedures manual has been written and distributed,   4.____

    A. continuous maintenance work is necessary to keep the manual current
    B. it is best to issue new manuals rather than make changes in the original manual
    C. no changes should be necessary
    D. only major changes should be considered

5. Of the following, the MOST important criterion of effective report writing is   5.____

    A. eloquence of writing style
    B. the use of technical language
    C. to be brief and to the point
    D. to cover all details

6. The use of electronic data processing   6.____

    A. has proven unsuccessful in most organizations
    B. has unquestionable advantages for all organizations
    C. is unnecessary in most organizations
    D. should be decided upon only after careful feasibility studies by individual organizations

7. Of the following methods, which would normally be MOST appropriate to validate a new aptitude test?   7.____

    A. Concurrent   B. Construct
    C. Content   D. Predictive

71

8. The PRIMARY purpose of work measurement is to

   A. design and install a wage incentive program
   B. determine who should be promoted
   C. establish a yardstick to determine extent of progress
   D. set up a spirit of competition among employees

9. A hypothetical construct is BEST defined as an(any)

   A. speculation that a researcher wishes to articulate
   B. entity or process presumed to exist but currently unable to be observed
   C. explanation of what antecedent conditions lead to various consequences
   D. expression of the relationship between stimulus and response variables

10. Representative samples are

    A. always drawn from finite populations
    B. always drawn from infinite populations
    C. drawn in a random, unbiased manner and have the characteristics of the larger universe
    D. larger than stratified samples

11. Interval or equal-interval scales have

    A. an absolute or natural zero that has empirical meaning
    B. none of the characteristics of nominal and ordinal scales
    C. no validity
    D. the property that numerically equal distances on the scale represent equal distances in the property being measured

12. Protective techniques of obtaining and analyzing information from respondents are

    A. designed so that subjects will respond as frankly as possible
    B. easier to analyze than objective techniques
    C. forms of structured scales
    D. to be avoided at all costs

13. Of the following, which is NOT a descriptive research design? _____ study.

    A. Case
    B. Correlation
    C. Developmental
    D. Pretest-posttest

14. One method of testing hypotheses using available materials produced by institutions, organizations, and individuals is

    A. content analysis
    B. distance-cluster analysis
    C. semantic differential
    D. sociometric analysis

15. The MOST important difference between experimental research and ex post facto research is

    A. analysis of data required
    B. control of the variables
    C. cost of the study
    D. length of time required to conduct the study

16. The public health department of a large city wishes to study the effect of different chemicals on the retardation of tooth decay in children. Three groups of children ranging in age from 10 to 15 are selected randomly. One group of children is given toothpaste containing chemical X and another group is given toothpaste with chemical Y. A third group is given toothpaste with no chemical added. All three groups are given the same kind of toothbrush and are asked to brush their teeth twice a day for one year using the toothpaste and toothbrushes they have received. Periodic dental check-ups are made of the children in all three groups to determine the amount of tooth decay.
    In the above study, the independent and dependent variables may BEST be defined as follows:

    A. chemicals X and Y and toothbrushes are independent variables and the amount of tooth decay is the dependent variable
    B. chemicals X and Y are independent variables and the amount of tooth decay is the dependent variable
    C. chemicals X and Y, toothbrushes, and the number of times a day the children brush their teeth are dependent variables and the amount of tooth decay is the independent variable
    D. chemicals X and Y, toothbrushes, and the number of times a day the children brush their teeth are independent variables and the amount of tooth decay is the dependent variable

17. A research hypothesis may BEST be defined as a(n)

    A. problem statement concerning two or more unknown variables
    B. speculation based on the researcher"s experience
    C. statement of expectation concerning the relations between variables which can be tested
    D. expository statement of the statistical procedure to be used in the research

18. A review of the literature is included in the research report PRIMARILY in order to

    A. demonstrate the scope of the investigator's knowledge about the research problem
    B. develop the theoretical foundation of the study
    C. indicate the literature reviewed by the investigator in planning the study
    D. save the reader time

19. The null hypothesis is a statistical proposition which states that

    A. no explanation of differences between variables should be accepted completely
    B. no differences exist between two or more sample means
    C. no variable can be accurately measured
    D. the real difference between the variables of the problem is greater than one would expect by chance

20. The following scores were obtained by an elementary mathematics class at the end of one year of instruction:

11	19	17
2	15	6
5	6	8

    If the score of 8 were changed to 10, the mean(,)
    A. and median of this group of data would change but the mode would remain the same
    B. median, and mode would change
    C. median, and mode would remain the same
    D. of this group of data would change but the median would remain the same

    20.____

21. The normal distribution which is represented by a theoretical bell-shaped curve has the following property:

    A. Exactly .6826 of the total area will fall between an ordinate of two standard deviations above the mean
    B. It is a fictional curve having no real function
    C. The mean and median will coincide and have exactly the same value
    D. The total area under the curve is equal to 2.98

    21.____

22. In the case of variables that are linearly related, the correlation coefficient is a measure of

    A. the causal relationship present between variables
    B. the difference between the mean and the standard deviation
    C. the direction and degree of the relationship between variables
    D. which variable is independent and which is dependent

    22.____

23. If a student's score on the final examination in a chemistry class is at the 72nd percentile, one can SAFELY assume that

    A. the student answered 7 more questions correctly than did a student whose score was at the 65th percentile
    B. 72% of the class scored lower than this student
    C. the student answered 72 out of 100 questions correctly
    D. the student is above average in chemistry

    23.____

24. The significance level of a statistic is the probability that

    A. a Type II error has been committed
    B. the obtained result of the statistic could occur by chance
    C. the outcome of the experiment is $\overline{X}_1 \neq \overline{X}_2$
    D. there is a positive relationship between the variables being measured

    24.____

25. The standard error of the mean is an estimate of

    A. how far the sample mean is likely to differ from the population mean
    B. how far two sample means differ from each other
    C. the amount of error committed in computation
    D. the amount of error inherent in the population mean

    25.____

26. Nonparametric statistics are different from parametric statistics in that 26.____

    A. conditions about the population parameters are not specified in nonparametric tests
    B. nonparametric statistics are easier and faster to compute
    C. the measures to be analyzed by nonparametric tests must be continuous
    D. the measures to be analyzed by parametric statistics must be discrete

27. The Chi square test CANNOT be used reliably when the 27.____

    A. population distribution is not assumed to be normal
    B. population distribution is positively skewed
    C. samples are very large
    D. samples are very small

28. Of the following, the MOST critical problem faced by metropolitan educational systems is 28.____

    A. inadequate physical facilities
    B. parental indifference
    C. the lack of motivation to learn among urban youth
    D. the rapidity and magnitude of population change

29. In reference to educational systems, the concept of community control 29.____

    A. advocates that parents should take the place of professional educators
    B. implies that all educational decisions should be voted upon in open community meetings
    C. is essentially the same as decentralization
    D. represents the idea that the ultimate authority to make policy decisions rests with community representatives

30. Of the following, the MOST serious drawback to the *grant-in-aid* approach to support community services is that 30.____

    A. grants are difficult to obtain
    B. it encourages overcentralization of services
    C. it has had little or no provision for coordination of services
    D. it is too expensive

31. Of the following, the BEST definition of records management is 31.____

    A. storage of all types of records at minimum expense
    B. planned control of all types of records
    C. storage of records for maximum accessibility
    D. systematic filing of all types of records

32. The title of a contemporary best-selling book by Robert Townsend is . 32.____

    A. MANAGEMENT ANALYSIS: WAVE OF THE FUTURE
    B. MANAGEMENT FOR RESULTS
    C. THE HUMAN SIDE OF ENTERPRISE
    D. UP THE ORGANIZATION

33. A summary punched card containing totals of a group of similar detail cards is GENER-   33.____
ALLY called a _____ card.

   A. master unit record
   B. summary unit record
   C. total
   D. unit record

34. One of the more famous studies of organizations is called the Hawthorne study.   34.____
This work was one of the first to point out the importance of

   A. employees' benefit and retirement programs
   B. informal organization among employees
   C. job engineering
   D. styles of position classification

35. In organization theory, the type of position in which an individual is appointed to give   35.____
technical aid to management on a particular problem area is generally BEST termed a(n)

   A. administrative assistant
   B. *assistant to*
   C. staff assistant
   D. staff specialist

36. In analyzing data for the acquisition of new equipment, a methods analyst gathers the   36.____
facts, analyzes them, and develops new procedures which will be required when the new
equipment arrives.
In analyzing the factors involved, which one of the following is normally LEAST important in the evaluation of new equipment?

   A. Cost factors
   B. Layout and installation factors
   C. Production planning
   D. Operational experience of manufacturers of allied equipment

37. The one of the following which is NOT a primary objective of a records retention and dis-   37.____
posal system is to

   A. assure appropriate preservation of records having permanent value
   B. dispose of records not warranting further preservation
   C. establish retention standards for archives
   D. provide an opportunity to use miniaturization techniques to simplify filing systems

38. In organizing, doing what *works* in the particular situation, with due regard to both short   38.____
and long range objectives, is BEST termed

   A. ambivalence
   B. authoritarianism
   C. decentralization
   D. pragmatism

39. If an effort were made to reduce the number of private offices in a new layout, the LEAST   39.____
effective substitute in offering privacy would be the use of

   A. an open area, with lower movable partitions or railings separating each individual
   B. conference rooms
   C. larger desks
   D. modular desk units

40. The term *administrative substation* NORMALLY refers to 40.____
    A. a work station handling a number of office services for an office organization
    B. a work station where middle level supervisors are located
    C. an office for handling management trainees
    D. the functions allocated to particular levels of administrative managers

KEY (CORRECT ANSWERS)

1.	A	11.	D	21.	C	31.	B
2.	A	12.	A	22.	C	32.	D
3.	B	13.	D	23.	B	33.	B
4.	A	14.	A	24.	B	34.	B
5.	C	15.	B	25.	A	35.	D
6.	D	16.	B	26.	A	36.	D
7.	D	17.	C	27.	D	37.	D
8.	C	18.	B	28.	D	38.	D
9.	B	19.	B	29.	D	39.	C
10.	C	20.	A	30.	C	40.	A

TEST 2

DIRECTIONS: Each question or incomplete statement is followed by several suggested answers or completions. Select the one that BEST answers the question or completes the statement. *PRINT THE LETTER OF THE CORRECT ANSWER IN THE SPACE AT THE RIGHT.*

1. A research technique which would be applied to determine the optimum number of window clerks or interviewers to have in an agency serving the public would MOST likely be the use of

    A. line of balance
    B. queuing theory
    C. simulation
    D. work sampling

2. A type of file which permits the operator to remain seated while the file can be moved backward and forward as required is BEST termed a file.

    A. lateral
    B. movable
    C. reciprocating
    D. rotary

3. The technique of work measurement in which the analyst observes the work at random times of the day is BEST termed

    A. indirect observation
    B. logging
    C. ratio delay
    D. wristwatch

4. Examples of predetermined time systems generally should include all of the following EXCEPT

    A. Master Clerical Data
    B. Methods Time Measurement
    C. Short Interval Data
    D. Work Factor

5. A technique by which the supervisor or an assistant distributes a predetermined batch of work to the employees at periodic intervals of the day is generally BEST known as

    A. backlog control scheduling
    B. production control scheduling
    C. short interval scheduling
    D. workload balancing

6. Wright Bakke defined his *fusion process* as the

    A. work environment to some degree remakes the organization and the organization to some degree remakes the work environment
    B. fusing of the interests of both management and labor unions
    C. community of interest between first line supervisors and top management
    D. organization to some degree remakes the individual and the individual to some degree remakes the organization

7. If a staff analyst is required to recommend the selection of a machine for an office operation, he can BEST judge the expected output of a particular machine by pursuing which of the following courses of action?
Obtaining

    A. an actual test run of the machine in his office
    B. data from the manufacturer of the machine
    C. information on the percentage of working time the machine will be used
    D. the experience of actual users of similar machines elsewhere

8. In planning office space for a newly established bureau, it would usually be LEAST desirable to

   A. concentrate, rather than disperse, the chief sources of office noises
   B. design an office environment with about the same brightness as the office desk
   C. designate as reception rooms, washrooms, and other service areas those areas that will receive lesser amounts of illumination than those areas in which private office work will be performed
   D. eliminate natural light in cases where it is not the major light source

9. A private office should be used when its use is dictated by facts and unbiased judgment. It should never be provided simply because requests and sometimes pressure have been brought to bear.
   Of the following reasons used to justify use of a private office, the one that requires the MOST care in determining whether a private office is actually warranted is

   A. an office has always been provided for a particular job
   B. prestige considerations
   C. the confidential nature of the work
   D. the work involves high concentration

10. Theoretically, an ideal organization structure can be set up for each enterprise. In actual practice, the ideal organization structure is seldom, if ever, obtained.
    Of the following, the one that normally is of LEAST influence in determining the organization structure is the

    A. existence of agreements and favors among members of the organization
    B. funds available
    C. opinions and beliefs of top executives
    D. tendency of management to discard established forms in favor of new forms

11. An IMPORTANT aspect to keep in mind during the decision-making process is that

    A. all possible alternatives for attaining goals should be sought out and considered
    B. considering various alternatives only leads to confusion
    C. once a decision has been made, it cannot be retracted
    D. there is only one correct method to reach any goal

12. Implementation of accountability requires

    A. a leader who will not hesitate to take punitive action
    B. an established system of communication from the bottom to the top
    C. explicit directives from leaders
    D. too much expense to justify it

13. Of the following, the MAJOR difference between systems and procedures analysis and work simplification is

    A. the former complicates organizational routine and the latter simplifies it
    B. the former is objective and the latter is subjective
    C. the former generally utilizes expert advice and the latter is a *do-it-yourself* improvement by supervisors and workers
    D. there is no difference other than in name

14. Systems development is concerned with providing

    A. a specific set of work procedures
    B. an overall framework to describe general relationships
    C. definitions of particular organizational functions
    D. organizational symbolism

15. Organizational systems and procedures should be

    A. developed as problems arise as no design can anticipate adequately the requirements of an organization
    B. developed jointly by experts in systems and procedures and the people who are responsible for implementing them
    C. developed solely by experts in systems and procedures
    D. eliminated whenever possible to save unnecessary expense

16. The CHIEF danger of a decentralized control system is that

    A. excessive reports and communications will be generated
    B. problem areas may not be detected readily
    C. the expense will become prohibitive
    D. this will result in too many *chiefs*

17. Of the following, management guides and controls clerical work PRINCIPALLY through

    A. close supervision and constant checking of personnel
    B. spot checking of clerical procedures
    C. strong sanctions for clerical supervisors
    D. the use of printed forms

18. Which of the following is MOST important before conducting fact-finding interviews?

    A. Becoming acquainted with all personnel to be interviewed
    B. Explaining the techniques you plan to use
    C. Explaining to the operating officials the purpose and scope of the study
    D. Orientation of the physical layout

19. Of the following, the one that is NOT essential in carrying out a comprehensive work improvement program is

    A. standards of performance   B. supervisory training
    C. work count/task list   D. work distribution chart

20. Which of the following control techniques is MOST useful on large, complex systems projects?

    A. A general work plan   B. Gantt Chart
    C. Monthly progress report   D. PERT Chart

21. The action which is MOST effective in gaining acceptance of a study by the agency which is being studied is

    A. a directive from the agency head to install a study based on recommendations included in a report
    B. a lecture-type presentation following approval of the procedures
    C. a written procedure in narrative form covering the proposed system with visual presentations and discussions
    D. procedural charts showing the *before* and *after* situation, forms, steps, etc. to the employees affected

22. Which of the following is NOT an advantage in the use of oral instructions as compared with written instructions? Oral instruction(s)

    A. can easily be changed
    B. is superior in transmitting complex directives
    C. facilitate exchange of information between a superior and his subordinate
    D. without discussions make it easier to ascertain understanding

23. Which organization principle is MOST closely related to procedural analysis and improvement?

    A. Duplication, overlapping, and conflict should be eliminated.
    B. Managerial authority should be clearly defined.
    C. The objectives of the organization should be clearly defined.
    D. Top management should be freed of burdensome detail.

24. Which of the following is the MAJOR objective of operational audits?

    A. Detecting fraud
    B. Determining organization problems
    C. Determining the number of personnel needed
    D. Recommending opportunities for improving operating and management practices

25. Of the following, the formalization of organization structure is BEST achieved by

    A. a narrative description of the plan of organization
    B. functional charts
    C. job descriptions together with organization charts
    D. multi-flow charts

26. Budget planning is MOST useful when it achieves

    A. cost control
    B. forecast of receipts
    C. performance review
    D. personnel reduction

27. The underlying principle of sound administration is to

    A. base administration on investigation of facts
    B. have plenty of resources available
    C. hire a strong administrator
    D. establish a broad policy

28. Although questionnaires are not the best survey tool the management analyst has to use, there are times when a good questionnaire can expedite the *fact-finding* phase of a management survey.
    Which of the following should be AVOIDED in the design and distribution of the questionnaire?

    A. Questions should be framed so that answers can be classified and tabulated for analysis.
    B. Those receiving the questionnaire must be knowledgeable enough to accurately provide the information desired.
    C. The questionnaire should enable the respondent to answer in a narrative manner.
    D. The questionnaire should require a minimum amount of writing.

28.____

29. Of the following, the formula which is used to calculate the arithmetic mean from data grouped in a frequency distribution is

    A. $M = \dfrac{N}{\Sigma fX}$
    B. $M = N(\Sigma fX)$
    C. $M = \dfrac{\Sigma fX}{N}$
    D. $M = \dfrac{\Sigma X}{fN}$

29.____

30. Arranging large groups of numbers in frequency distributions

    A. gives a more composite picture of the total group than a random listing
    B. is misleading in most cases
    C. is unnecessary in most instances
    D. presents the data in a form whereby further manipulation of the group is eliminated

30.____

31. After a budget has been developed, it serves to

    A. assist the accounting department in posting expenditures
    B. measure the effectiveness of department managers
    C. provide a yardstick against which actual costs are measured
    D. provide the operating department with total expenditures to date

31.____

32. Of the following, which formula is used to determine staffing requirements?

    A. $\dfrac{\text{Hours per man-day}}{\text{Volume X Standard}} = \text{Employees Needed}$
    B. $\dfrac{\text{Hours per man-day X Standard}}{\text{Volume}} = \text{Employees Needed}$
    C. $\dfrac{\text{Hours per man-day X Volume}}{\text{Standard}} = \text{Employees Needed}$
    D. $\dfrac{\text{Volume X Standard}}{\text{Hours per man-day}} = \text{Employees Needed}$

32.____

33. Of the following, which formula is used to determine the number of days required to process work?

33.____

A. $\dfrac{\text{Employees} \times \text{Daily Output}}{\text{Volume}} = \text{Days to Process Work}$

B. $\dfrac{\text{Employees} \times \text{Volume}}{\text{Daily Output}} = \text{Days to Process Work}$

C. $\dfrac{\text{Volume}}{\text{Employees} \times \text{Daily Output}} = \text{Days to Process Work}$

D. $\dfrac{\text{Volume} \times \text{Daily Output}}{\text{Employees}} = \text{Days to Process Work}$

34. Identify this symbol, as used in a Systems Flow Chart.
    A. Document
    B. Decision
    C. Preparation
    D. Process

35. Of the following, the MAIN advantage of a form letter over a dictated letter is that a form letter

    A. is more expressive
    B. is neater
    C. may be mailed in a window envelope
    D. requires less secretarial time

36. The term that may be defined as a systematic analysis of all factors affecting work being done or all factors that will affect work to be done, in order to save effort, time or money is

    A. flow process charting   B. work flow analysis
    C. work measurement   D. work simplification

37. Generally, the LEAST important basic factor to be considered in developing office layout improvements is to locate

    A. office equipment, reference facilities, and files as close as practicable to those using them
    B. persons as close as practicable to the persons from whom they receive their work
    C. persons as close as practicable to windows and/or adequate ventilation
    D. persons who are friendly with each other close together to improve morale

38. Of the following, the one which is LEAST effective in reducing administrative costs is

    A. applying objective measurement techniques to determine the time required to perform a given task
    B. establishing budgets on the basis of historical performance data
    C. motivating supervisors and managers in the importance of cost reduction
    D. selecting the best method - manual, mechanical, or electronic - to process the essential work

39. *Fire-fighting* is a common expression in management terminology.
Of the following, which BEST describes *fire-fighting* as an analyst's approach to solving paperwork problems?

   A. A complete review of all phases of the department's processing functions
   B. A studied determination of the proper equipment to process the work
   C. An analysis of each form that is being processed and the logical reasons for its processing
   D. The solution of problems as they arise, usually at the request of operating personnel

40. Assume that an analyst with a proven record of accomplishment on many projects is having difficulties on his present assignment.
Of the following, the BEST course of action for his superior to take is to

   A. assume there is a personality conflict involved and transfer the analyst to another project
   B. give the analyst some time off
   C. review the nature of the project to determine whether or not the analyst is equipped to handle the assignment
   D. suggest that the analyst seek counseling

KEY (CORRECT ANSWERS)

1. B	11. A	21. C	31. C
2. C	12. B	22. B	32. D
3. C	13. C	23. A	33. C
4. C	14. B	24. D	34. A
5. C	15. B	25. C	35. D
6. D	16. B	26. A	36. D
7. A	17. D	27. A	37. D
8. D	18. C	28. C	38. B
9. A	19. B	29. C	39. D
10. D	20. D	30. A	40. C

SUPERVISION, ADMINISTRATION, MANAGEMENT, AND ORGANIZATION

EXAMINATION SECTION

TEST 1

DIRECTIONS: Each question or incomplete statement is followed by several suggested answers or completions. Select the one that BEST answers the question or completes the statement. *PRINT THE LETTER OF THE CORRECT ANSWER IN THE SPACE AT THE RIGHT.*

1. In coaching a subordinate on the nature of decision-making, an executive would be right if he stated that the one of the following which is general the BEST definition of decision-making is:
   A. Choosing between alternatives
   B. Making diagnoses of feasible ends
   C. Making diagnoses of feasible means
   D. Comparing alternatives

   1.____

2. Of the following, which one would be LEAST valid as a purpose of an organizational policy statement?
   To
   A. keep personnel from performing improper actions and functions on routine matters
   B. prevent the mishandling of non-routine matters
   C. provide management personnel with a tool that precludes the need for their use of judgment
   D. provide standard decisions and approaches in handling problems of a recurrent nature

   2.____

3. Much has been written criticizing bureaucratic organizations. Current thinking on the subject is GENERALLY that
   A. bureaucracy is on the way out
   B. bureaucracy, though not perfect, is unlikely to be replaced
   C. bureaucratic organizations are most effective in dealing with constant change
   D. bureaucratic organizations are most effective when dealing with sophisticated customers or clients

   3.____

4. The development of alternate plans as a major step in planning will normally result in the planner having several possible courses of action available.
   GENERALLY, this is
   A. *desirable*, since such development helps to determine the most suitable alternative and to provide for the unexpected
   B. *desirable*, since such development makes the use of planning premises and constraints unnecessary

   4.____

C. *undesirable*, since the planners should formulate only one way of achieving given goals at a given time
D. *undesirable*, since such action restricts efforts to modify the planning to take advantage of opportunities

5. The technique of departmentation by task force includes the assigning of a team or task force to a definite project or block of work which extends from the beginning to the completing of a wanted and definite type and quantity of work. Of the following, the MOST important actor aiding the successful use of this technique *normally* is
   A. having the task force relatively large, at least one hundred members
   B. having a definite project termination date established
   C. telling each task force member what his next assignment will be only after the current project ends
   D. utilizing it only for projects that are regularly recurring

5.____

6. With respect to communication in small group settings such as may occur in business, government, and the military, it is generally TRUE that people usually derive more satisfaction and are usually more productive under conditions which
   A. permit communication only with superiors
   B. permit the minimum intragroup communication possible
   C. are generally restricted by management
   D. allow open communication among all group members

6.____

7. If an executive were asked to list some outstanding features of decentralization, which one of the following would NOT be such a feature?
   Decentralization
   A. provides decision-making experience for lower level managers
   B. promotes uniformity of policy
   C. is a relatively new concept in management
   D. is similar to the belief in encouragement of free enterprise

7.____

8. Modern management experts have emphasized the importance of the informal organization in motivating employees to increase productivity.
   Of the following, the characteristic which would have the MOST direct influence on employee motivation is the tendency of members of the informal organization to
   A. resist change
   B. establish their own norms
   C. have similar outside interests
   D. set substantially higher goals than those of management

8.____

9. According to leading management experts, the decision-making process contains separate and distinct steps that must be taken in an orderly sequence.
   Of the following arrangements, which one is in CORRECT order?

9.____

A. I. Search for alternatives; II. diagnosis; III. comparison; IV. choice
B. I. Diagnose; II. comparison; III. search for alternatives; IV. choice
C. I. Diagnose; II. search for alternatives; III. comparison; IV. choice
D. I. Diagnose; II. search for alternatives; III. choice; IV. comparison

10. Of the following, the growth of professionalism in large organizations can PRIMARILY be expected to result in
    A. greater equalization of power
    B. increased authoritarianism
    C. greater organizational disloyalty
    D. increased promotion opportunities

10.____

11. Assume an executive carries out his responsibilities to his staff according to what is now known about managerial leadership.
    Which of the following statements would MOST accurately reflect his assumptions about proper management?
    A. Efficiency in operations results from allowing the human element to participate in a minimal way.
    B. Efficient operation result from balancing work considerations with personnel considerations.
    C. Efficient operation results from a workforce committed to its self-interest.
    D. Efficient operation results from staff relationships that produce a friendly work climate.

11.____

12. Assume that an executive is called upon to conduct a management audit. To do this properly, he would have to take certain steps in a specific sequence.
    Of the following steps, which step should this manager take FIRST?
    A. Managerial performance must be surveyed.
    B. A method of reporting must be established.
    C. Management auditing procedures and documentation must be developed.
    D. Criteria for the audit must be considered.

12.____

13. If a manager is required to conduct a scientific investigation of an organizational problem, the FIRST step he should take is to
    A. state his assumptions about the problem
    B. carry out a search for background information
    C. choose the right approach to investigate the validity of his assumptions
    D. define and state the problem

13.____

14. An executive would be right to assert that the principle of delegation states that decisions should be made PRIMARILY
    A. by persons in an executive capacity qualified to make them
    B. by persons in a non-executive capacity
    C. at as low an organization level of authority as practicable
    D. by the next lower level of authority

14.____

15. Of the following, which one is NOT regarded by management authorities as a FUNDAMENTAL characteristic of an *ideal* bureaucracy?
    A. Division of labor and specialization
    B. An established hierarchy
    C. Decentralization of authority
    D. A set of operating rules and regulations

16. As the number of subordinates in a manager's span of control increases, the ACTUAL number of possible relationships
    A. increases disproportionately to the number of subordinates
    B. increases in equal number to the number of subordinates
    C. reaches a stable level
    D. will first increase then slowly decrease

17. An executive's approach to controlling the activities of his subordinates concentrated on ends rather than means, and was diagnostic rather than punitive.
    This manager may MOST properly be characterized as using the managerial technique of management-by-
    A. exception   B. objectives   C. crisis   D. default

18. In conducting a training session on the administrative control process, which of the following statements would be LEAST valid for an executive to make? Controlling
    A. requires checking upon assignments to see what is being done
    B. involves comparing what is being done to what ought to be done
    C. requires corrective action when what is being done does not meet expectations
    D. occurs after all the other managerial processes have been performed

19. The "brainstorming" technique for creative solutions of management problems MOST generally consists of
    A. bringing staff together in an exchange of a quantity of freewheeling ideas
    B. isolating individual staff members to encourage thought
    C. developing improved office procedures
    D. preparation of written reports on complex problems

20. Computer systems hardware MOST often operates in relation to which one of the following steps in solving a data-processing problem?
    A. Determining the problem
    B. Defining and stating the problem
    C. Implementing the programmed solution
    D. Completing the documentation of every unexplored solution

21. There is a tendency in management to upgrade objectives.
    This trend is generally regarded as
    A. *desirable*; the urge to improve is demonstrated by adopting objectives that have been adjusted to provide improved service

B. *undesirable*; the typical manager searches for problems which obstruct his objectives
C. *desirable*; it is common for a manager to find that the details of an immediate operation have occupied so much of his time that he has lost sight of the basic overall objective
D. *undesirable*; efforts are wasted when they are expended on a mass of uncertain objectives, since the primary need of most organizations is a single target or several major ones

22. Of the following, it is generally LEAST effective for an executive to delegate authority where working conditions involve
    A. rules establishing normal operating procedures
    B. consistent methods of operation
    C. rapidly changing work standards
    D. complex technology

23. If an executive was explaining the difficulty of making decisions under *risk* conditions, he would be MOST accurate if he said that such decisions would be difficult to make when the decision maker has _____ information and experience and can expect _____ outcomes for each action.
    A. limited; many
    B. much; many
    C. much; few
    D. limited; few

24. If an executive were asked to list some outstanding features of centralized organization, which one of the following would be INCORRECT?
    Centralized organization
    A. lessens risks of errors by unskilled subordinates
    B. utilizes the skills of specialized experts at a central location
    C. produces uniformity of policy and non-uniformity of action
    D. enables closer control of operations than a decentralized set-up

25. It is possible for an organization's management to test whether or not the organization has a sound structure.
    Of the following, which one is NOT a test of soundness in an organization's structure?
    The
    A. ability to replace key personnel with minimum loss of effectiveness
    B. ability of information and decisions to flow more freely through the *grapevine* than through formal channels
    C. provision for orderly organizational growth with the ability to handle change as the need arises.

KEY (CORRECT ANSWERS)

1.	A	11.	B
2.	C	12.	D
3.	B	13.	D
4.	A	14.	C
5.	B	15.	C
6.	D	16.	A
7.	B	17.	B
8.	B	18.	D
9.	C	19.	A
10.	A	20.	C

21.	A
22.	C
23.	A
24.	C
25.	B

TEST 2

DIRECTIONS: Each question or incomplete statement is followed by several suggested answers or completions. Select the one that BEST answers the question or completes the statement. *PRINT THE LETTER OF THE CORRECT ANSWER IN THE SPACE AT THE RIGHT.*

1. Management experts generally believe that computer-based management information systems (MIS) have greater potential for improving the process of management than any other development in recent decades.
   The one of the following which MOST accurately describes the objectives of MIS is to
   A. provide information for decision-making on planning, initiating, and controlling the operations of the various units of the organization
   B. establish mechanization of routine functions such as clerical records, payroll, inventory, and accounts receivable in order to promote economy and efficiency
   C. computerize decision-making on planning, initiative, organizing, and controlling the operations of an organization
   D. provide accurate facts and figures on the various programs of the organization to be used for purposes of planning and research

   1.____

2. The one of the following which is the BEST application on the *management-by-exception* principle is that this principle
   A. stimulates communication and aids in management of crisis situations, thus reducing the frequency of decision-making
   B. saves time and reserves top-management decisions only for crisis situations, thus reducing the frequency of decision-making
   C. stimulates communication, saves time, and reduces the frequency of decision-making
   D. is limited to crisis-management situations

   2.____

3. It is generally recognized that each organization is dependent upon availability of qualified personnel.
   Of the following, the MOST important factor affecting the availability of qualified people to each organization is
   A. innovations in technology and science
   B. the general decline in the educational levels of our population
   C. the rise of sentiment against racial discrimination
   D. pressure by organized community groups

   3.____

4. A fundamental responsibility of all managers is to decide what physical facilities and equipment are needed to help attain basic goals.
   Good planning for the purchase and use of equipment is seldom easy to do and is complicated MOST by the fact that
   A. organizations rarely have stable sources of supply
   B. nearly all managers tend to be better at personnel planning than at equipment planning

   4.____

C. decisions concerning physical resources are made too often on a *crash basis* rather than under carefully prepared policies
D. legal rulings relative to depreciation fluctuate very frequently

5. In attempting to reconcile managerial objectives and an individual employee's goals, it is generally LEAST desirable for management to
   A. recognize the capacity of the individual to contribute toward realization of managerial goals
   B. encourage self-development of the employee to exceed minimum job performance
   C. consider an individual employee's work separately from other employees
   D. demonstrate that an employee advances only to the extent that he contributes directly to the accomplishment of stated goals

6. As a management tool for discovering individual training needs a job analysis would generally be of LEAST assistance in determining
   A. the performance requirements of individual jobs
   B. actual employee performance on the job
   C. acceptable standards of performance
   D. training needs for individual jobs

7. One of the major concerns of organizational managers today is how the spread of automation will affect them and the status of their positions. Realistically speaking, one can say that the MOST likely effect of our newer forms of highly automated technology on managers will be to
   A. make most top-level positions superfluous or obsolete
   B. reduce the importance of managerial work in general
   C. replace the work of managers with the work of technicians
   D. increase the importance of and demand for top managerial personnel

8. Which one of the following is LEAST likely to be an area or cause of trouble in the use of staff people (e.g., assistants to the administrator)?
   A. Misunderstanding of the role the staff people are supposed to play, as a result of vagueness of definition of their duties and authority
   B. Tendency of staff personnel almost always to be older than line personnel at comparable salary levels with who they must deal
   C. Selection of staff personnel who fail to have simultaneously both competence in their specialties and skill in staff work
   D. The staff person fails to understand mixed staff and operating duties

9. The one of the following which is the BEST measure of decentralization in an agency is the
   A. amount of checking required on decisions made at lower levels in the chain of command
   B. amount of checking required on decisions made at lower levels of the chain of command and the number of functions affected thereby
   C. number of functions affected by decisions made at higher levels
   D. number of functions affected by middle echelon decision-making

10. Which of the following is generally NOT a valid statement with respect to the supervisory process?
    A. General supervision is more effective than close supervision.
    B. Employee-centered supervisors lead more effectively than do production-centered supervisors.
    C. Employee satisfaction is directly related to productivity.
    D. Low-producing supervisors use techniques that are different from high-producing supervisors.

11. The one of the following which is the MOST essential element for proper evaluation of the performance of subordinate supervisors is a
    A. careful definition of each supervisor's specific job responsibilities and of his progress in meeting mutually agreed upon work goals
    B. system of rewards and penalties based on each supervisor's progress in meeting clearly defined performance standards
    C. definition of personality traits, such as industry, initiative, dependability, and cooperativeness, required for effective job performance
    D. breakdown of each supervisor's job into separate components and a rating of his performance on each individual task

12. The one of the following which is the PRINCIPAL advantage of specialization for the operating efficiency of a public service agency is that specialization
    A. reduces the amount of red tape in coordinating the activities of mutually dependent departments
    B. simplifies the problem of developing adequate job controls
    C. provides employees with a clear understanding of the relationship of their activities to the overall objectives of the agency
    D. reduces destructive competition for power between departments

13. Of the following, the group which generally benefits MOST from supervisory training programs in public service agencies are those supervisors who have
    A. accumulated a long period of total service to the agency
    B. responsibility for a large number of subordinate personnel
    C. been in the supervisory ranks for a long period of time
    D. a high level of formalized academic training

14. A list of conditions which encourages good morale inside a work group would NOT include a
    A. high rate of agreement among group members on values and objectives
    B. tight control system to minimize the risk of individual error
    C. good possibility that joint action will accomplish goals
    D. past history of successful group accomplishment

15. Of the following, the MOST important factor to be considered in selecting a training strategy or program is the
    A. requirements of the job to be performed by the trainees
    B. educational level or prior training of the trainees
    C. size of the training group
    D. quality and competence of available training specialists

16. Of the following, the one which is considered to be LEAST characteristic of the higher ranks of management is
    A. that higher levels of management benefit from modern technology
    B. that success is measured by the extent to which objectives are achieved
    C. the number of subordinates that directly report to an executive
    D. the de-emphasis of individual and specialized performance

17. Assume that an executive is preparing a training syllabus to be used in training members of his staff.
    Which of the following would NOT be a valid principle of the learning process for this manager to keep in mind in the preparation of the training syllabus?
    A. When a person has thoroughly learned a task, it takes a lot of effort to create a little more improvement.
    B. In complicated learning situations, there is a period in which an additional period of practice produces an equal amount of improvement in learning.
    C. The less a person knows about the task, the slower the initial progress.
    D. The more the person knows about the risk, the slower the initial progress.

18. Of the following, which statement BEST illustrates when collective bargaining agreements are working well?
    A. Executives strongly support subordinate managers.
    B. The management rights clause in the contract is clear and enforced.
    C. Contract provisions are competently interpreted.
    D. The provisions of the agreement are properly interpreted, communicated, and observed.

19. An executive who wishes to encourage subordinates to communicate freely with him about a job-related problem should FIRST
    A. state his own position on the problem before listening to the subordinates' ideas
    B. invite subordinates to give their own opinions on the problem
    C. ask subordinates for their reactions to his own ideas about the problem
    D. guard the confidentiality of management information about the problem

20. The ability to deal constructively with intra-organizational conflict is an essential attribute of the successful manager.
    The one of the following types of conflict which would be LEAST difficult to handle constructively is a situation in which there is
    A. agreement on objectives, but disagreement as to the probable results of adopting the various alternatives
    B. agreement on objectives, disagreement on alternative courses of action, and relative certainty as to the outcome of one of the alternatives
    C. disagreement on objectives and on alternate courses of action, but relative certainty as to the outcome of the alternatives
    D. disagreement on objectives and on alternative course of action, but uncertainty as to the outcome of the alternatives

5 (#2)

21. Which of the following statements is LEAST accurate in describing formal job evaluation and wage and salary classification plans? 21.____
    A. Parties that disagree on wage matters can examine an established system rather than unsupported opinions.
    B. The use of such plans tends to overlook the effect of age and seniority of employees on job values in the plan.
    C. Such plans can eliminate salary controversies in organizations designing and using them properly.
    D. These plans are not particularly useful in checking on executive compensation.

22. In carrying out disciplinary action, the MOST important procedure for all managers to follow is to 22.____
    A. sell all levels of management on the need for discipline from the organization's viewpoint
    B. follow up on a disciplinary action and not assume that the action has been effective
    C. convince all executives that proper discipline is a legitimate tool for their use
    D. convince all executives that they need to display confidence in the organization's rules

Questions 23-25.

DIRECTIONS: Questions 23 through 25 are to be answered on the basis of the following situation. Richard Ford, a top administrator, is responsible for output in his organization. Because productivity had been lagging for two periods in a row, Ford decided to establish a committee of his subordinate managers to investigate the reasons for the poor performance and to make recommendations for improvements. After two meetings, the committee came to the conclusions and made the recommendations that follow:

Output forecasts had been handed down from the top without prior consultation with middle management and first level supervision. Lines of authority and responsibility had been unclear. The planning and control process should be decentralized.
After receiving the committee's recommendations, Ford proceeded to take the following actions:
Ford decided he would retain final authority to establish quotas but would delegate to the middle managers the responsibility for meeting quotas.
After receiving Ford's decision, the middle managers proceeded to delegate to the first-line supervisors the authority to establish their own quotas. The middle managers eventually received and combined the first-line supervisors' quotas so that these conformed with Ford's.

23. Ford's decision to delegate responsibility for meeting quotas to the middle managers is INCONSISTENT with sound management principles because of which one of the following? 23.____
    A. Ford shouldn't have involved himself in the first place.
    B. Middle managers do not have the necessary skills.

C. Quotas should be established by the chief executive.
D. Responsibility should not be delegated.

24. The principle of co-extensiveness of responsibility and authority bears on Ford's decision.   24.____
In this case, it IMPLIES that
    A. authority should exceed responsibility
    B. authority should be delegated to match the degree of responsibility
    C. both authority and responsibility should be retained and not delegated
    D. responsibility should be delegated but authority should be retained

25. The middle manager's decision to delegate to the first-line supervisors the authority to establish quotas was INCORRECTLY reasoned because   25.____
    A. delegation and control must go together
    B. first-line supervisors are in no position to establish quotas
    C. one cannot delegate authority that one does not possess
    D. the meeting of quotas should not be delegated

KEY (CORRECT ANSWERS)

1.	A		11.	A
2.	C		12.	B
3.	A		13.	D
4.	C		14.	B
5.	C		15.	A
6.	B		16.	C
7.	D		17.	D
8.	B		18.	D
9.	B		19.	B
10.	C		20.	B

21. C
22. B
23. D
24. B
25. C

TEST 3

DIRECTIONS: Each question or incomplete statement is followed by several suggested answers or completions. Select the one that BEST answers the question or completes the statement. *PRINT THE LETTER OF THE CORRECT ANSWER IN THE SPACE AT THE RIGHT.*

1. A danger which exists in any organization as complex as that required for administration of a large public agency is that each department comes to believe that it exists for its own sake.
   The one of the following which has been attempted in some organizations as a cure for this condition is to
   A. build up the departmental esprit de corps
   B. expand the functions and jurisdictions of the various departments so that better integration is possible
   C. develop a body of specialists in the various subject matter fields which cut across departmental lines
   D. delegate authority to the lowest possible echelon
   E. systematically transfer administrative personnel from one department to another

2. At best, the organization chart is ordinarily and necessarily an idealized picture of the intent of top management, a reflection of hopes and aims rather than a photograph of the operating facts within the organization.
   The one of the following which is the basic reason for this is that the organization chart
   A. does not show the flow of work within the organization
   B. speaks in terms of positions rather than of live employees
   C. frequently contains unresolved internal ambiguities
   D. is a record of past organization or proposed future organization and never a photograph of the living organization
   E. does not label the jurisdiction assigned to each component unit

3. The drag of inadequacy is always downward. The need in administration is always for the reverse; for a department head to project his thinking to the city level, for the unit chief to try to see the problems of the department.
   The inability of a city administration to recruit administrators who can satisfy this need usually results in departments characterized by
   A. disorganization   B. poor supervision
   C. circumscribed viewpoints   D. poor public relations
   E. a lack of programs

4. When, as a result of a shift in public sentiment, the elective officers of a city are changed, is it desirable for career administrators to shift ground without performing any illegal or dishonest act in order to conform to the policies of the new elective officers?
   A. *No;* the opinions and beliefs of the career officials are the result of long experience in administration and are more reliable than those of politicians

B. *Yes*; only in this way can citizens, political officials, and career administrators alike have confidence in the performance of their respective functions
C. *No*; a top career official who is so spineless as to change his views or procedures as a result of public opinion is of little value to the public service
D. *Yes*; legal or illegal, it is necessary that a city employee carry out the orders of his superior officers
E. *No*; shifting ground with every change in administration will preclude the use of a constant overall policy

5. Participation in developing plans which will affect levels in the organization in addition to his own, will contribute to an individual's understanding of the entire system. When possible, this should be encouraged.
   This policy is, in general,
   A. *desirable*; the maintenance of any organization depends upon individual understanding
   B. *undesirable*; employees should participate only in these activities which affect their own level, otherwise conflicts in authority may arise
   C. *desirable*; an employee's will to contribute to the maintenance of an organization depends to a great extent on the level which he occupies
   D. *undesirable*; employees can be trained more efficiently and economically in an organized training program than by participating in plan development
   E. *desirable*; it will enable the employee to make intelligent suggestions for adjustment of the plan in the future

5.____

6. Constant study should be made of the information contained in reports to isolate those elements of experience which are static, those which are variable and repetitive, and those which are variable and due to chance.
   Knowledge of those elements of experience in his organization which are static or constant will enable the operating official to
   A. fix responsibility for their supervisor at a lower level
   B. revise the procedure in order to make the elements variable
   C. arrange for follow-up and periodic adjustment
   D. bring related data together
   E. provide a frame of reference within which detailed standards for measurement can be installed

6.____

7. A chief staff officer, serving as one of the immediate advisors to the department head, has demonstrated a special capacity for achieving internal agreements and for sound judgment. As a result he has been used more and more as a source of counsel and assistance by the department head. Other staff officers and line officials as well have discovered that it is wise for them to check with this colleague in advance on all problematical matters handed up to the department head.

7.____

Developments such as this are
- A. *undesirable*; they disrupt the normal lines for flow of work in an organization
- B. *desirable*; they allow an organization to make the most of its strength wherever such strength resides
- C. *undesirable*; they tend to undermine the authority of the department head and put it in the hands of a staff officer who does not have the responsibility
- D. *desirable*; they tend to resolve internal ambiguities in organization
- E. *undesirable*; they make for bad morale by causing *cutthroat* competition

8. A common difference among executives is that some are not content unless they are out in front of everything that concerns their organization, while others prefer to run things by pulling strings, by putting others out in front and by stepping into the breach only when necessary.
Generally speaking, an advantage this latter method of operation has over the former is that it
    - A. results in a higher level of morale over a sustained period of time
    - B. gets results by exhortation and direct stimulus
    - C. makes it unnecessary to calculate integrated moves
    - D. makes the personality of the executive felt further down the line
    - E. results in the executive getting the reputation for being a good fellow

8.____

9. Administrators frequently have to get facts by interviewing people. Although the interview is a legitimate fact gathering technique, it has definite limitations which should not be overlooked.
The one of the following which is an important limitation is that
    - A. people who are interviewed frequently answer questions with guesses rather than admit their ignorance
    - B. it is a poor way to discover the general attitude and thinking of supervisors interviewed
    - C. people sometimes hesitate to give information during an interview which they will submit in written form
    - D. it is a poor way to discover how well employees understand departmental policies
    - E. the material obtained from the interview can usually be obtained at lower cost from existing records

9.____

10. It is desirable and advantageous to leave a maximum measure of planning responsibility to operating agencies or units, rather than to remove the responsibility to a central planning staff agency.
Adoption of the former policy (decentralized planning) would lead to
    - A. *less effective planning*; operating personnel do not have the time to make long-term plans
    - B. *more effective planning*; operating units are usually better equipped technically than any staff agency and consequently are in a better position to set up valid plans
    - C. *less effective planning*; a central planning agency has a more objective point of view than any operating agency can achieve

10.____

D. *more effective planning*; plans are conceived in terms of the existing situation and their execution is carried out with the will to succeed
E. *less effective planning*; there is little or no opportunity to check deviation from plans in the proposed set-up

Questions 11-15.

DIRECTIONS: The following sections appeared in a report on the work production of two bureaus of a department. Base your answers to Questions 11 through 15 on this information. Throughout the report, assume that each month has 4 weeks.

Each of the two bureaus maintains a chronological file. In Bureau A, every 9 months on the average, this material fills a standard legal size cabinet sufficient for 12,000 work units. In Bureau B the same type of cabinet is filled in 18 months. Each bureau maintains three complete years of information plus a current file. When the current file cabinet is filled, the cabinet containing the oldest material is emptied, the contents disposed of, and the cabinet used for current material. The similarity of these operations makes it possible to consolidate these files with little effort.

Study of the practice of using typists as filing clerks for periods when there is no typing work showed: (1) Bureau A has for the past 6 months completed a total of 1,500 filing work units a week using on the average 100 man-hours of trained file clerk time and 20 man-hours of typist time; (2) Bureau B has in the same period completed a total of 2,000 filing work units a week using on the average 125 man-hours of trained file clerk time and 60 hours of typist time. This includes all work in chronological files. Assuming that all clerks work at the same speed and that all typists work at the same speed, this indicates that work other than filing should be found for typists or that they should be given some training in the filing procedures used. It should be noted that Bureau A has not been producing the 1,600 units of technical (not filing) work per 30-day period required by Schedule K, but is at present 200 units behind. The Bureau should be allowed 3 working days to get on schedule.

11. What percentage (approximate) of the total number of filing work units completed in both units consists of the work involved in the maintenance of the chronological files?
    A. 5%   B. 10%   C. 15%   D. 20%   E. 25%

12. If the two chronological files are consolidated, the number of months which should be allowed for filling a cabinet is
    A. 2   B. 4   C. 6   D. 8   E. 14

13. The MAXIMUM number of file cabinets which can be released for other uses as a result of the consolidation recommended is
    A. 0
    B. 1
    C. 2
    D. 3
    E. not determinable on the basis of the data given

14. If all the filing work for both units is consolidated without diminution in the amount to be done and all filing work is done by trained file clerks, the number of clerks required (35-hour work week) is

    A. 4 B. 5 C. 6 D. 7 E. 8

    14.____

15. In order to comply with the recommendation with respect to Schedule K, the present work production of Bureau A must be increased by

    A. 50%
    B. 100%
    C. 150%
    D. 200%
    E. an amount which is not determinable

    15.____

16. A certain training program during World War II resulted in the training of thousands of supervisors in industry. The methods of this program were later successfully applied in various government agencies. The program was based upon the assumption that there is an irreducible minimum of three supervisory skills.
    The one of these skills among the following is
    A. to know how to perform the job at hand well
    B. to be able to deal personally with workers, especially face-to-face
    C. to be able to imbue workers with the will to perform the job well
    D. to know the kind of work that is done by one's unit and the policies and procedures of one's agency
    E. the *know-how* of administrative and supervisory processes

    16.____

17. A comment made by an employee about a training course was, "*We never have any idea how we ae getting along in that course.*"
    The fundamental error in training methods to which this criticism points is
    A. insufficient student participation
    B. failure to develop a feeling of need or active want for the material being presented
    C. the training sessions may be too long
    D. no attempt may have been made to connect the new material with what was already known
    E. no goals have been set for the students

    17.____

18. Assume that you are attending a departmental conference on efficiency ratings at which it is proposed that a man-to-man rating scale be introduced.
    You should point out that, of the following, the CHIEF weakness of the man-to-man rating scale is that
    A. it involves abstract numbers rather than concrete employee characteristics
    B. judges are unable to select their own standards for comparison
    C. the standard for comparison shifts from man-to-man for each person rated
    D. not every person rated is given the opportunity to serve as a standard for comparison
    E. standards for comparison will vary from judge to judge

    18.____

19. Assume that you are conferring with a supervisor who has assigned to his subordinates efficiency ratings which you believe to be generally too low. The supervisor argues that his ratings are generally low because his subordinates are generally inferior.
Of the following, the evidence MOST relevant to the point at issue can be secured by comparing efficiency ratings assigned by the supervisor
    A. with ratings assigned by other supervisors in the same agency
    B. this year with ratings assigned by him in previous years
    C. to men recently transferred to his unit with ratings previously earned by these men
    D. with the general city average of ratings assigned by all supervisors to all employees
    E. with the relative order of merit of his employees as determined independently by promotion test marks

19._____

20. The one of the following which is NOT among the most common of the compensable factors used in wage evaluation studies is
    A. initiative and ingenuity required
    B. physical demand
    C. responsibility for the safety of others
    D. working conditions
    E. presence of avoidable hazards

20._____

21. If independent functions are separated, there is an immediate gain in conserving special skills. If we are to make optimum use of the abilities of our employees, these skills must be conserved.
Assuming the correctness of this statement, it follows that
    A. if we are not making optimum use of employee abilities, independent functions have not been separated
    B. we are making optimum uses of employee abilities if we conserve special skills
    C. we are making optimum use of employee abilities if independent functions have been separated
    D. we are not making optimum use of employee abilities if we do not conserve special skills
    E. if special skills are being conserved, independent functions need not be separated

21._____

22. A reorganization of the bureau to provide for a stenographic pool instead of individual unit stenographers will result in more stenographic help being available to each unit when it is required, and consequently will result in greater productivity for each unit. An analysis of the space requirements shows that setting up a stenographic pool will require a minimum of 400 square feet of good space. In order to obtain this space, it will be necessary to reduce the space available for technical personnel, resulting in lesser productivity for each unit.

22._____

On the basis of the above discussion, it can be stated that, in order to obtain greater productivity for each unit,
- A. a stenographic pool should be set up
- B. further analysis of the space requirement should be made
- C. it is not certain as to whether or not a stenographic pool should be set up
- D. the space available for each technician should be increased in order to compensate for the absence of a stenographic pool
- E. a stenographic pool should not be set up

23. The adoption of single consolidated form will mean that most of the form will not be used in any one operation. This would create waste and confusion. This conclusion is based upon the unstated hypothesis that
    - A. if waste and confusion are to be avoided, a single consolidated form should be used
    - B. if a single consolidated form is constructed, most of it can be used in each operation
    - C. if waste and confusion are to be avoided, most of the form employed should be used
    - D. most of a single consolidation form is not used
    - E. a single consolidated form should not be used

23.____

KEY (CORRECT ANSWERS)

1.	E		11.	C
2.	B		12.	C
3.	C		13.	B
4.	B		14.	D
5.	E		15.	E
6.	A		16.	B
7.	B		17.	E
8.	A		18.	E
9.	A		19.	C
10.	D		20.	E

21.	D
22.	C
23.	C

COMMUNICATION
EXAMINATION SECTION
TEST 1

DIRECTIONS: Each question or incomplete statement is followed by several suggested answers or completions. Select the one that BEST answers the question or completes the statement. *PRINT THE LETTER OF THE CORRECT ANSWER IN THE SPACE AT THE RIGHT.*

1. In some agencies the counsel to the agency head is given the right to bypass the chain of command and issue orders directly to the staff concerning matters that involve certain specific processes and practices.
   This situation MOST nearly illustrates the principle of _____ authority.
   A. the acceptance theory of
   B. multiple-linear
   C. splintered
   D. functional

   1.____

2. It is commonly understood that communication is an important part of the administrative process.
   Which of the following is NOT a valid principle of the communication process in administration?
   A. The channels of communication should be spontaneous.
   B. The lines of communication should be as direct and as short as possible.
   C. Communications should be authenticated.
   D. The persons serving in communications centers should be competent.

   2.____

3. Of the following, the one factor which is generally considered LEAST essential to successful committee operations is
   A. stating a clear definition of the authority and scope of the committee
   B. selecting the committee chairman carefully
   C. limiting the size of the committee to four persons
   D. limiting the subject matter to that which can be handled in group discussion

   3.____

4. Of the following, the failure by line managers to accept and appreciate the benefits and limitations of a new program or system VERY FREQUENTLY can be traced to the
   A. budgetary problems involved
   B. resultant need to reduce staff
   C. lack of controls it engenders
   D. failure of top management to support its implementation

   4.____

5. If a manager were thinking about using a committee of subordinates to solve an operating problem, which of the following would generally NOT be an advantage of such use of the committee approach?
   A. Improved coordination
   B. Low cost
   C. Increased motivation
   D. Integrated judgment

   5.____

6. Every supervisor has many occasions to lead a conference or participate in a conference of some sort.
Of the following statements that pertain to conferences and conference leadership, which is generally considered to be MOST valid?
   A. Since World War II, the trend has been toward fewer shared decisions and more conferences.
   B. The most important part of a conference leader's job is to direct discussion.
   C. In providing opportunities for group interaction, management should avoid consideration of its past management philosophy.
   D. A good administrator cannot lead a good conference if he is a poor public speaker.

7. Of the following, it is usually LEAST desirable for a conference leader to
   A. call the name of a person after asking a question
   B. summarize proceedings periodically
   C. make a practice of repeating questions
   D. ask a question without indicating who is to reply

8. Assume that, in a certain organization, a situation has developed in which there is little difference in status or authority between individuals.
Which of the following would be the MOST likely result with regard to communication in this organization?
   A. Both the accuracy and flow of communication will be improved.
   B. Both the accuracy and flow of communication will substantially decrease.
   C. Employees will seek more formal lines of communication.
   D. Neither the flow nor the accuracy of communication will be improved over the former hierarchical structure.

9. The main function of many agency administrative officers is "information management." Information that is received by an administrative officer may be classified as active or passive, depending upon whether or not it requires the recipient to take some action.
Of the following, the item received which is clearly the MOST active information is
   A. an appointment of a new staff member
   B. a payment voucher for a new desk
   C. a press release concerning a past event
   D. the minutes of a staff meeting

10. Of the following, the one LEAST considered to be a communication barrier is
   A. group feedback   B. charged words
   C. selective perception   D. symbolic meanings

11. Management studies support the hypothesis that, in spite of the tendency of employees to censor the information communicated to their supervisor, subordinates are more likely to communicate problem-oriented information UPWARD when they have a
    A. long period of service in the organization
    B. high degree of trust in the supervisor
    C. high educational level
    D. low status on the organizational ladder

11.____

12. Electronic data processing equipment can produce more information faster than can be generated by any other means.
In view of this, the MOST important problem faced by management at present is to
    A. keep computers fully occupied
    B. find enough computer personnel
    C. assimilate and properly evaluate the information
    D. obtain funds to establish appropriate information systems

12.____

13. A well-designed management information system essentially provides each executive and manager the information he needs for
    A. determining computer time requirements
    B. planning and measuring results
    C. drawing a new organization chart
    D. developing a new office layout

13.____

14. It is generally agreed that management policies should be periodically reappraised and restated in accordance with current conditions.
Of the following, the approach which would be MOST effective in determining whether a policy should be revised is to
    A. conduct interviews with staff members at all levels in order to ascertain the relationship between the policy and actual practice
    B. make proposed revisions in the policy and apply it to current problems
    C. make up hypothetical situations using both the old policy and a revised version in order to make comparisons
    D. call a meeting of top level staff in order to discuss ways of revising the policy

14.____

15. Your superior has asked you to notify division employees of an important change in one of the operating procedures described in the division manual. Every employee presently has a copy of this manual.
Which of the following is normally the MOST practical way to get the employees to understand such a change?
    A. Notify each employee individually of the change and answer any questions he might have
    B. Send a written notice to key personnel, directing them to inform the people under them

15.____

C. Call a general meeting, distribute a corrected page for the manual, and discuss the change
D. Send a memo to employees describing the change in general terms and asking them to make the necessary corrections in their copies of the manual

16. Assume that the work in your department involves the use of any technical terms.
In such a situation, when you are answering inquiries from the general public, it would usually be BEST to
    A. use simple language and avoid the technical terms
    B. employ the technical terms whenever possible
    C. bandy technical terms freely, but explain each term in parentheses
    D. apologize if you are forced to use a technical term

17. Suppose that you receive a telephone call from someone identifying himself as an employee in another city department who asks to be given information which your own department regards as confidential.
Which of the following is the BEST way of handling such a request?
    A. Give the information requested, since your caller as official standing
    B. Grant the request, provided the caller gives you a signed receipt
    C. Refuse the request, because you have no way of knowing whether the caller is really who he claims to be
    D. Explain that the information is confidential and inform the caller of the channels he must go through to have the information released to him

18. Studies show that office employees place high importance on the social and human aspects of the organization. What office employees like best about their jobs is the kind of people with whom they work. So strive hard to group people who are most likely to get along well together.
Based on this information, it is MOST reasonable to assume that office workers are most pleased to work in a group which
    A. is congenial
    B. has high productivity
    C. allows individual creativity
    D. is unlike other groups

19. A certain supervisor does not compliment members of his staff when they come up with good ideas. He feels that coming up with good ideas is part of the job and does not merit special attention.
This supervisor's practice is
    A. *poor*, because recognition for good ideas is a good motivator
    B. *poor*, because the staff will suspect that the supervisor has no good ideas of his own
    C. *good*, because it is reasonable to assume that employees will tell their supervisor of ways to improve office practice
    D. *good*, because the other members of the staff are not made to seem inferior by comparison

20. Some employees of a department have sent an anonymous letter containing many complaints to the department head.
Of the following, what is this MOST likely to show about the department?
    A. It is probably a good place to work.
    B. Communications are probably poor.
    C. The complaints are probably unjustified.
    D. These employees are probably untrustworthy.

20.____

21. Which of the following actions would usually be MOST appropriate for a supervisor to take after receiving an instruction sheet from his superior explaining a new procedure which is to be followed?
    A. Put the instruction sheet aside temporarily until he determines what is wrong with the old procedure.
    B. Call his superior and ask whether the procedure is one he must implement immediately.
    C. Write a memorandum to the superior asking for more details.
    D. Try the new procedure and advise the superior of any problems or possible improvements.

21.____

22. Of the following, which one is considered the PRIMARY advantage of using a committee to resolved a problem in an organization?
    A. No one person will be held accountable for the decision since a group of people was involved.
    B. People with different backgrounds give attention to the problem.
    C. The decision will take considerable time so there is unlikely to be a decision that will later be regretted.
    D. One person cannot dominate the decision-making process.

22.____

23. Employees in a certain office come to their supervisor with all their complaints about the office and the work. Almost every employee has had at least one minor complaint at some time.
The situation with respect to complaints in this office may BEST be described as probably
    A. *good*; employees who complain care about their jobs and work hard
    B. *good*; grievances brought out into the open can be corrected
    C. *bad*; only serious complaints should be discussed
    D. *bad*; it indicates the staff does not have confidence in the administration

23.____

24. The administrator who allows his staff to suggest ways to do their work will usually find that
    A. this practice contributes to high productivity
    B. the administrator's ideas produce greater output
    C. clerical employees suggest inefficient work methods
    D. subordinate employees resent performing a management function

24.____

25. The MAIN purpose for a supervisor's questioning the employees at a conference he is holding is to
    A. stress those areas of information covered but not understood by the participants
    B. encourage participants to think through the problem under discussion
    C. catch those subordinates who are not paying attention
    D. permit the more knowledgeable participants to display their grasp of the problems being discussed

25._____

KEY (CORRECT ANSWERS)

1.	D		11.	B
2.	A		12.	C
3.	C		13.	B
4.	D		14.	A
5.	B		15.	C
6.	B		16.	A
7.	C		17.	D
8.	D		18.	A
9.	A		19.	A
10.	A		20.	B

21. D
22. B
23. B
24. A
25. B

TEST 2

DIRECTIONS: Each question or incomplete statement is followed by several suggested answers or completions. Select the one that BEST answers the question or completes the statement. *PRINT THE LETTER OF THE CORRECT ANSWER IN THE SPACE AT THE RIGHT.*

1. For a superior to use *consultative supervision* with his subordinates effectively, it is ESSENTIAL that he
    A. accept the fact that his formal authority will be weakened by the procedure
    B. admit that he does not know more than all his men together and that his ideas are not always best
    C. utilize a committee system so that the procedure is orderly
    D. make sure that all subordinates are consulted so that no one feels left out

2. The *grapevine* is an informal means of communication in an organization. The attitude of a supervisor with respect to the grapevine should be to
    A. ignore it since it deals mainly with rumors and sensational information
    B. regard it as a serious danger which should be eliminated
    C. accept it as a real line of communication which should be listened to
    D. utilize it for most purposes instead of the official line of communication

3. The supervisor of an office that must deal with the public should realize that planning in this type of work situation
    A. is useless because he does not know how many people will request service or what service they will request
    B. must be done at a higher level but that he should be ready to implement the results of such planning
    C. is useful primarily for those activities that are not concerned with public contact
    D. is useful for all the activities of the office, including those that relate to public contact

4. Assume that it is your job to receive incoming telephone calls. Those calls which you cannot handle yourself have to be transferred to the appropriate office.
    If you receive an outside call for an extension line which is busy, the one of the following which you should do FIRST is to
    A. interrupt the person speaking on the extension and tell him a call is waiting
    B. tell the caller the line is busy and let him know every thirty seconds whether or not it is free
    C. leave the caller on "hold" until the extension is free
    D. tell the caller the line is busy and ask him if he wishes to wait

5. Your superior has subscribed to several publications directly related to your division's work, and he has asked you to see to it that the publications are circulated among the supervisory personnel in the division. There are eight supervisors involved.
   The BEST method of insuring that all eight see these publications is to
   A. place the publication in the division's general reference library as soon as it arrives
   B. inform each supervisor whenever a publication arrives and remind all of them that they are responsible for reading it
   C. prepare a standard slip that can be stapled to each publication, listing the eight supervisors and saying, "Please read, initial your name, and pass along"
   D. send a memo to the eight supervisors saying that they may wish to purchase individual subscriptions in their own names if they are interested in seeing each issue

6. Your superior has telephoned a number of key officials in your agency to ask whether they can meet at a certain time next month. He has found that they can all make it, and he has asked you to confirm the meeting.
   Which of the following is the BEST way to confirm such a meeting?
   A. Note the meeting on your superior's calendar.
   B. Post a notice of the meeting on the agency bulletin board.
   C. Call the officials on the day of the meeting to remind them of the meeting.
   D. Write a memo to each official involved, repeating the time and place of the meeting.

7. Assume that a new city regulation requires that certain kinds of private organizations file information forms with your department. You have been asked to write the short explanatory message that will be printed on the front cover of the pamphlet containing the forms and instructions.
   Which of the following would be the MOST appropriate way of beginning this message?
   A. Get the readers' attention by emphasizing immediately that there are legal penalties for organizations that fail to file before a certain date.
   B. Briefly state the nature of the enclosed forms and the types of organizations that must file.
   C. Say that your department is very sorry to have to put organizations to such an inconvenience.
   D. Quote the entire regulation adopted by the city, even if it is quite long and is expressed din complicated legal language.

8. Suppose that you have been told to make up the vacation schedule for the 18 employees in a particular unit. In order for the unit to operate effectively, only a few employees can be on vacation at the same time.
   Which of the following is the MOST advisable approach in making up the schedule?
   A. Draw up a schedule assigning vacations in alphabetical order
   B. Find out when the supervisors want to take their vacations, and randomly assign whatever periods are left to the non-supervisory personnel

C. Assign the most desirable times to employees of longest standing and the least desirable times to the newest employees
D. Have all employees state their own preference, and then work out any conflicts in consultation with the people involved

9. Assume that you have been asked to prepare job descriptions for various positions in your department.
Which of the following are the basic points that should be covered in a *job description*?
   A. General duties and responsibilities of the position, with examples of day-to-day tasks
   B. Comments on the performances of present employees
   C. Estimates of the number of openings that may be available in each category during the coming year
   D. Instructions for carrying out the specific tasks assigned to your department

10. Of the following, the biggest DISADVANTAGE in allowing a free flow of communications in an agency is that such a free flow
    A. decreases creativity
    B. increases the use of the *grapevine*
    C. lengthens the chain of command
    D. reduces the executive's power to direct the flow of information

11. A downward flow of authority in an organization is one example of _____ communication.
    A. horizontal   B. informal   C. circular   D. vertical

12. Of the following, the one that would MOST likely block effective communication is
    A. concentration only on the issues at hand
    B. lack of interest or commitment
    C. use of written reports
    D. use of charts and graphs

13. An ADVANTAGE of the *lecture* as a teaching tool is that it
    A. enables a person to present his ideas to a large number of people
    B. allows the audience to retain a maximum of the information given
    C. holds the attention of the audience for the longest time
    D. enables the audience member to easily recall the main points

14. An ADVANTAGE of the *small-group* discussion as a teaching tool is that
    A. it always focuses attention on one person as the leader
    B. it places collective responsibility on the group as a whole
    C. its members gain experience by summarizing the ideas of others
    D. each member of the group acts as a member of a team

15. The one of the following that is an ADVANTAGE of a *large-group* discussion, when compared to a small-group discussion, is that the large-group discussion
    A. moves along more quickly than a small-group discussion
    B. allows its participants to feel more at ease, and speak out more freely
    C. gives the whole group a chance to exchange ideas on a certain subject at the same occasion
    D. allows its members to feel a greater sense of personal responsibility

15.____

KEY (CORRECT ANSWERS)

1. D	6. D	11. D
2. C	7. B	12. B
3. D	8. D	13. A
4. D	9. A	14. D
5. C	10. D	15. C

PRINCIPLES AND PRACTICES, OF ADMINISTRATION, SUPERVISION AND MANAGEMENT

TABLE OF CONTENTS

	Page
GENERAL ADMINISTRATION	1
SEVEN BASIC FUNCTIONS OF THE SUPERVISOR	2
I. Planning	2
II. Organizing	3
III. Staffing	3
IV. Directing	3
V. Coordinating	3
VI. Reporting	3
VII. Budgeting	3
PLANNING TO MEET MANAGEMENT GOALS	4
I. What is Planning	4
II. Who Should Make Plans	4
III. What are the Results of Poor Planning	4
IV. Principles of Planning	4
MANAGEMENT PRINCIPLES	5
I. Management	5
II. Management Principles	5
III. Organization Structure	6
ORGANIZATION	8
I. Unity of Command	8
II. Span of Control	8
III. Uniformity of Assignment	9
IV. Assignment of Responsibility and Delegation of Authority	9
PRINCIPLES OF ORGANIZATION	9
I. Definition	9
II. Purpose of Organization	9
III. Basic Considerations in Organizational Planning	9
IV. Bases for Organization	10
V. Assignment of Functions	10
VI. Delegation of Authority and Responsibility	10
VII. Employee Relationships	11

DELEGATING		11
I.	WHAT IS DELEGATING:	11
II.	TO WHOM TO DELEGATE	11
REPORTS		12
I.	DEFINITION	12
II.	PURPOSE	12
III.	TYPES	12
IV.	FACTORS TO CONSIDER BEFORE WRITING REPORT	12
V.	PREPARATORY STEPS	12
VI.	OUTLINE FOR A RECOMMENDATION REPORT	12
MANAGEMENT CONTROLS		13
I.	Control	13
II.	Basis for Control	13
III.	Policy	13
IV.	Procedure	14
V.	Basis of Control	14
FRAMEWORK OF MANAGEMENT		14
I.	Elements	14
II.	Manager's Responsibility	15
III.	Control Techniques	16
IV.	Where Forecasts Fit	16
PROBLEM SOLVING		16
I.	Identify the Problem	16
II.	Gather Data	17
III.	List Possible Solutions	17
IV.	Test Possible Solutions	18
V.	Select the Best Solution	18
VI.	Put the Solution into Actual Practice	19
COMMUNICATION		19
I.	What is Communication?	19
II.	Why is Communication Needed?	19
III.	How is Communication Achieved?	20
IV.	Why Does Communication Fail?	21
V.	How to Improve Communication	21
VI.	How to Determine If You Are Getting Across	21
VII.	The Key Attitude	22
HOW ORDERS AND INSTRUCTIONS SHOULD BE GIVEN		22
I.	Characteristics of Good Orders and Instructions	22
FUNCTIONS OF A DEPARTMENT PERSONNEL OFFICE		23

SUPERVISION	23
I. Leadership	23
A. The Authoritarian Approach	23
B. The Laissez-Faire Approach	24
C. The Democratic Approach	24
II. Nine Points of Contrast Between Boss and Leader	25
EMPLOYEE MORALE	25
I. Some Ways to Develop and Maintain Good Employee Morale	25
II. Some Indicators of Good Morale	26
MOTIVATION	26
EMPLOYEE PARTICIPATION	27
I. WHAT IS PARTICIPATION	27
II. WHY IS IT IMPORTANT?	27
III. HOW MAY SUPERVISORS OBTAIN IT?	28
STEPS IN HANDLING A GRIEVANCE	28
DISCIPLINE	29
I. THE DISCIPLINARY INTERVIEW	29
II. PLANNING THE INTERVIEW	29
III. CONDUCTING THE INTERVIEW	30

PRINCIPLES AND PRACTICES, OF
ADMINISTRATION, SUPERVISION AND MANAGEMENT

Most people are inclined to think of administration as something that only a few persons are responsible for in a large organization. Perhaps this is true if you are thinking of Administration with a capital A, but administration with a lower case *a* is a responsibility of supervisors at all levels each working day.

All of us feel we are pretty good supervisors and that we do a good job of administering the workings of our agency. By and large, this is true, but every so often it is good to check up on ourselves. Checklists appear from time to time in various publications which psychologists say tell whether or not a person will make a good wife, husband, doctor, lawyer, or supervisor.

The following questions are an excellent checklist to test yourself as a supervisor and administrator.

Remember, Administration gives direction and points the way but administration carries the ideas to fruition. Each is dependent on the other for its success. Remember, too, that no unit is too small for these departmental functions to be carried out. These statements apply equally as well to the Chief Librarian as to the Department Head with but one or two persons to supervise.

GENERAL ADMINISTRATION: General Responsibilities of Supervisors

1. Have I prepared written statements of functions, activities, and duties for my organizational unit?

2. Have I prepared procedural guides for operating activities?

3. Have I established clearly in writing, lines of authority and responsibility for my organizational unit?

4. Do I make recommendations for improvements in organization, policies, administrative and operating routines and procedures, including simplification of work and elimination of non-essential operations?

5. Have I designated and trained an understudy to function in my absence?

6. Do I supervise and train personnel within the unit to effectively perform their assignments?

7. Do I assign personnel and distribute work on such a basis as to carry out the organizational unit's assignment or mission in the most effective and efficient manner?

8. Have I established administrative controls by:

    a. Fixing responsibility and accountability on all supervisors under my direction for the proper performance of their functions and duties.

b. Preparations and submitting periodic work load and progress reports covering the operations of the unit to my immediate superior.

c. Analysis and evaluation of such reports received from subordinate units.

d. Submission of significant developments and problems arising within the organizational unit to my immediate superior.

e. Conducting conferences, inspections, etc., as to the status and efficiency of unit operations.

9. Do I maintain an adequate and competent working force?

10. Have I fostered good employee-department relations, seeing that established rules, regulations, and instructions are being carried out properly?

11. Do I collaborate and consult with other organizational units performing related functions to insure harmonious and efficient working relationships?

12. Do I maintain liaison through prescribed channels with city departments and other governmental agencies concerned with the activities of the unit?

13. Do I maintain contact with and keep abreast of the latest developments and techniques of administration (professional societies, groups, periodicals, etc.) as to their applicability to the activities of the unit?

14. Do I communicate with superiors and subordinates through prescribed organizational channels?

15. Do I notify superiors and subordinates in instances where bypassing is necessary as soon thereafter as practicable?

16. Do I keep my superior informed of significant developments and problems?

SEVEN BASIC FUNCTIONS OF THE SUPERVISOR

I. PLANNING
This means working out goals and means to obtain goals. <u>What</u> needs to be done, <u>who</u> will do it, <u>how</u>, <u>when</u>, and <u>where</u> it is to be done.

SEVEN STEPS IN PLANNING

A. Define job or problem clearly.
B. Consider priority of job.
C. Consider time-limit—starting and completing.
D. Consider minimum distraction to, or interference with, other activities.
E. Consider and provide for contingencies—possible emergencies.
F. Break job down into components.

G. Consider the 5 W's and H:
   WHY..........is it necessary to do the job? (Is the purpose clearly defined?)
   WHAT........needs to be done to accomplish the defined purpose?
          ....is needed to do the job? (Money, materials, etc.)
   WHO..........is needed to do the job?
          ....will have responsibilities?
   WHERE......is the work to be done?
   WHEN........is the job to begin and end? (Schedules, etc.)
   HOW..........is the job to bed done? (Methods, controls, records, etc.)

II. ORGANIZING

This means dividing up the work, establishing clear lines of responsibility and authority and coordinating efforts to get the job done.

III. STAFFING

The whole personnel function of bringing in and <u>training</u> staff, getting the right man and fitting him to the right job—the job to which he is best suited.

In the normal situation, the supervisor's responsibility regarding staffing normally includes providing accurate job descriptions, that is, duties of the jobs, requirements, education and experience, skills, physical, etc.; assigning the work for maximum use of skills; and proper utilization of the probationary period to weed out unsatisfactory employees.

IV. DIRECTING

Providing the necessary leadership to the group supervised. Important work gets done to the supervisor's satisfaction.

V. COORDINATING

The all-important duty of inter-relating the various parts of the work.
The supervisor is also responsible for controlling the coordinated activities. This means measuring performance according to a time schedule and setting quotas to see that the goals previously set are being reached. Reports from workers should be analyzed, evaluated, and made part of all future plans.

VI. REPORTING

This means proper and effective communication to your superiors, subordinates, and your peers (in definition of the job of the supervisor). Reports should be read and information contained therein should be used, not be filed away and forgotten. Reports should be written in such a way that the desired action recommended by the report is forthcoming.

VII. BUDGETING
This means controlling current costs and forecasting future costs. This forecast is based on past experience, future plans and programs, as well as current costs.

You will note that these seven functions can fall under three topics:

Planning) Make a plan	Staffing)	Reporting) Watch it work
Organizing)	Directing) Get things done	Budgeting)
	Controlling)	

PLANNING TO MEET MANAGEMENT GOALS

I. WHAT IS PLANNING?

    A. Thinking a job through before new work is done to determine the best way to do it
    B. A method of doing something
    C. Ways and means for achieving set goals
    D. A means of enabling a supervisor to deliver with a minimum of effort, all details involved in coordinating his work

II. WHO SHOULD MAKE PLANS?

Everybody!
All levels of supervision must plan work. (Top management, heads of divisions or bureaus, first line supervisors, and individual employees.) The higher the level, the more planning required.

III. WHAT ARE THE RESULTS OF POOR PLANNING?

    A. Failure to meet deadline
    B. Low employee morale
    C. Lack of job coordination
    D. Overtime is frequently necessary
    E. Excessive cost, waste of material and manhours

IV. PRINCIPLES OF PLANNING

    A. Getting a clear picture of your objectives. What exactly are you trying to accomplish?
    B. Plan the whole job, then the parts, in proper sequence.
    C. Delegate the planning of details to those responsible for executing them.
    D. Make your plan flexible.
    E. Coordinate your plan with the plans of others so that the work may be processed with a minimum of delay.
    F. Sell your plan before you execute it.
    G. Sell your plan to your superior, subordinate, in order to gain maximum participation and coordination.
    H. Your plan should take precedence. Use knowledge and skills that others have brought to a similar job.
    I. Your plan should take account of future contingencies; allow for future expansion.
    J. Plans should include minor details. Leave nothing to chance that can be anticipated.
    K. Your plan should be simple and provide standards and controls. Establish quality and quantity standards and set a standard method of doing the job. The controls will indicate whether the job is proceeding according to plan.
    L. Consider possible bottlenecks, breakdowns, or other difficulties that are likely to arise.

V. Q. WHAT ARE THE YARDSTICKS BY WHICH PLANNING SHOULD BE MEASURED?
    A. Any plan should:
    — Clearly state a definite course of action to be followed and goal to be achieved, with consideration for emergencies.
    — Be realistic and practical.
    — State what's to be done, when it's to be done, where, how, and by whom.
    — Establish the most efficient sequence of operating steps so that more is accomplished in less time, with the least effort, and with the best quality results.
    — Assure meeting deliveries without delays.
    — Establish the standard by which performance is to be judged.

    Q. WHAT KINDS OF PLANS DOES EFFECTIVE SUPERVISION REQUIRE?
    A. Plans should cover such factors as:
    — Manpower: right number of properly trained employees on the job
    — Materials: adequate supply of the right materials and supplies
    — Machines: full utilization of machines and equipment, with proper maintenance
    — Methods: most efficient handling of operations
    — Deliveries: making deliveries on time
    — Tools: sufficient well-conditioned tools
    — Layout: most effective use of space
    — Reports: maintaining proper records and reports
    — Supervision: planning work for employees and organizing supervisor's own time

MANAGEMENT PRINCIPLES

I. MANAGEMENT
    Q. What do we mean by management?
    A. Getting work done through others.

    Management could also be defined as planning, directing, and controlling the operations of a bureau or division so that all factors will function properly and all persons cooperate efficiently for a common objective.

II. MANAGEMENT PRINCIPLES

    A. There should be a hierarchy—wherein authority and responsibility run upward and downward through several levels—with a broad base at the bottom and a single head at the top.

    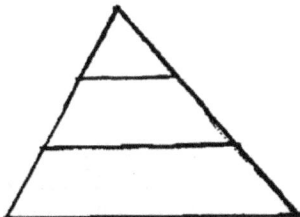

    B. Each and every unit or person in the organization should be answerable ultimately to the manager at the apex. In other words, *The buck stops here!*

C. Every necessary function involved in the bureau's objectives is assigned to a unit in that bureau.

D. Responsibilities assigned to a unit are specifically clear-cut and understood.

E. Consistent methods of organizational structure should be applied at each level of the organization.

F. Each member of the bureau from top to bottom knows: to whom he reports and who reports to him.

G. No member of one bureau reports to more than one supervisor. No dual functions.

H. Responsibility for a function is matched by authority necessary to perform that function. Weight of authority.

I. Individuals or units reporting to a supervisor do not exceed the number which can be feasibly and effectively coordinated and directed. Concept of *span of control.*

J. Channels of command (management) are not violated by staff units, although there should be staff services to facilitate and coordinate management functions.

K. Authority and responsibility should be decentralized to units and individuals who are responsible for the actual performance of operations.
Welfare – down to Welfare Centers
Hospitals – down to local hospitals

L. Management should exercise control through attention to policy problems of exceptional performance, rather than through review of routine actions of subordinates.

M. Organizations should never be permitted to grow so elaborate as to hinder work accomplishments.

III. ORGANIZATION STRUCTURE

Types of Organizations
The purest form is a leader and a few followers, such as:

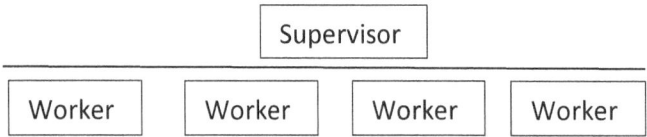

(Refer to organization chart) from supervisor to workers.

The line of authority is direct, The workers know exactly where they stand in relation to their boss, to whom they report for instructions and direction.

Unfortunately, in our present complex society, few organizations are similar to this example of a pure line organization. In this era of specialization, other people are often needed in the simplest of organizations. These specialists are known as staff. The sole purpose for their existence (staff) is to assist, advise, suggest, help or counsel line organizations. Staff has no authority to direct line people—nor do they give them direct instructions.

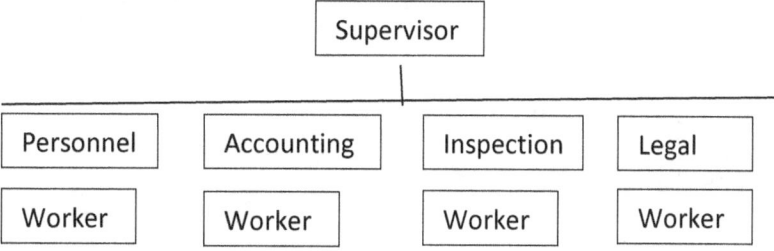

Line Functions
1. Directs
2. Orders
3. Responsibility for carrying out activities from beginning to end
4. Follows chain of command
5. Is identified with what it does
6. Decides when and how to use staff advice
7. Line executes

Staff Functions
1. Advises
2. Persuades and sells
3. Staff studies, reports, recommends but does not carry out
4. May advise across department lines
5. May find its ideas identified with others
6. Has to persuade line to want its advice
7. Staff: Conducts studies and research. Provides advice and instructions in technical matters. Serves as technical specialist to render specific services.

Types and Functions of Organization Charts
An organization chart is a picture of the arrangement and inter-relationship of the subdivisions of an organization.

A. Types of Charts:
   1. Structural: basic relationships only
   2. Functional: includes functions or duties
   3. Personnel: positions, salaries, status, etc.
   4. Process Chart: work performed
   5. Gantt Chart: actual performance against planned
   5. Flow Chart: flow and distribution of work

B. Functions of Charts:
   1. Assist in management planning and control
   2. Indicate duplication of functions
   3. Indicate incorrect stressing of functions
   4. Indicate neglect of important functions
   5. Correct unclear authority
   6. Establish proper span of control

C. Limitations of Charts:
   1. Seldom maintained on current basis
   2. Chart is oversimplified
   3. Human factors cannot adequately be charted

D. Organization Charts should be:
   1. Simple
   2. Symmetrical
   3. Indicate authority
   4. Line and staff relationship differentiated
   5. Chart should be dated and bear signature of approving officer
   6. Chart should be displayed, not hidden

ORGANIZATION

There are four basic principles of organization:
1. Unity of command
2. Span of control
3. Uniformity of assignment
4. Assignment of responsibility and delegation of authority

I. UNITY OF COMMAND

Unity of command means that each person in the organization should receive orders from one, and only one, supervisor. When a person has to take orders from two or more people, (a) the orders may be in conflict and the employee is upset because he does not know which he should obey, or (b) different orders may reach him at the same time and he does not know which he should carry out first.

Equally as bad as having two bosses is the situation where the supervisor is bypassed. Let us suppose you are a supervisor whose boss bypasses you (deals directly with people reporting to you). To the worker, it is the same as having two bosses; but to you, the supervisor, it is equally serious. Bypassing on the part of your boss will undermine your authority, and the people under you will begin looking to your boss for decisions and even for routine orders.

You can prevent bypassing by telling the people you supervise that if anyone tries to give them orders, they should direct that person to you.

II. SPAN OF CONTROL

Span of control on a given level involves:
A. The number of people being supervised
B. The distance
C The time involved in supervising the people. (One supervisor cannot supervise too many workers effectively.)

Span of control means that a supervisor has the right number (not too many and not too few) of subordinates that he can supervise well.

III. UNIFORMITY OF ASSIGNMENT

In assigning work, you as the supervisor should assign to each person jobs that are similar in nature. An employee who is assigned too many different types of jobs will waste time in going from one kind of work to another. It takes time for him to get to top production in one kind of task and, before he does so, he has to start on another.
When you assign work to people, remember that:

A. Job duties should be definite. Make it clear from the beginning <u>what</u> they are to do, <u>how</u> they are to do it, and <u>why</u> they are to do it. Let them know how much they are expected to do and how well they are expected to do it.
B. Check your assignments to be certain that there are no workers with too many unrelated duties, and that no two people have been given overlapping responsibilities. Your aim should be to have every task assigned to a specific person with the work fairly distributed and with each person doing his part.

IV. ASSIGNMENT OF RESPONSIBILITY AND DELEGATION OF AUTHORITY

A supervisor cannot delegate his final responsibility for the work of his department. The experienced supervisor knows that he gets his work done through people. He can't do it all himself. So he must assign the work and the responsibility for the work to his employees. Then they must be given the authority to carry out their responsibilities.

By assigning responsibility and delegating authority to carry out the responsibility, the supervisor builds in his workers initiative, resourcefulness, enthusiasm, and interest in their work. He is treating them as responsible adults. They can find satisfaction in their work, and they will respect the supervisor and be loyal to the supervisor.

PRINCIPLES OF ORGANIZATION

I. DEFINITION

Organization is the method of dividing up the work to provide the best channels for coordinated effort to get the agency's mission accomplished.

II. PURPOSE OF ORGANIZATION

A. To enable each employee within the organization to clearly know his responsibilities and relationships to his fellow employees and to organizational units
B. To avoid conflicts of authority and overlapping of jurisdiction.
C. To ensure teamwork.

III. BASIC CONSIDERATIONS IIN ORGANIZATIONAL PLANNING

A. The basic plans and objectives of the agency should be determined, and the organizational structure should be adapted to carry out effectively such plans and objectives.
B. The organization should be built around the major functions of the agency and not individuals or groups of individuals.

C. The organization should be sufficiently flexible to meet new and changing conditions which may be brought about from within or outside the department.
D. The organizational structure should be as simple as possible and the number of organizational units kept at a minimum.
E. The number of levels of authority should be kept at a minimum. Each additional management level lengthens the chain of authority and responsibility and increases the time for instructions to be distributed to operating levels and for decisions to be obtained from higher authority.
F. The form of organization should permit each executive to exercise maximum initiative within the limits of delegated authority.

IV. BASES FOR ORGANIZATION

A. Purpose (Examples: education, police, sanitation)
B. Process (Examples: accounting, legal, purchasing)
C. Clientele (Examples: welfare, parks, veteran)
D. Geographic (Examples: borough offices, precincts, libraries)

V. ASSIGNMENTS OF FUNCTIONS

A. Every function of the agency should be assigned to a specific organizational unit. Under normal circumstances, no single function should be assigned to more than one organizational unit.
B. There should be no overlapping, duplication, or conflict between organizational elements.
C. Line functions should be separated from staff functions, and proper emphasis should be placed on staff activities.
D. Functions which are closely related or similar should normally be assigned to a single organizational unit.
E. Functions should be properly distributed to promote balance, and to avoid overemphasis of less important functions and underemphasis of more essential functions.

VI. DELEGATION OF AUTHORITY AND RESPONSIBILITY

A. Responsibilities assigned to a specific individual or organizational unit should carry corresponding authority, and all statements of authority or limitations thereof should be as specific as possible.
B. Authority and responsibility for action should be decentralized to organizational units and individuals responsible for actual performance to the greatest extent possible, without relaxing necessary control over policy or the standardization of procedures. Delegation of authority will be consistent with decentralization of responsibility but such delegation will not divest an executive in higher authority of his overall responsibility.
C. The heads of organizational units should concern themselves with important matters and should delegate to the maximum extent details and routines performed in the ordinary course of business.
D. All responsibilities, authorities, and relationships should be stated in simple language to avoid misinterpretation.
E. Each individual or organizational unit charged with a specific responsibility will be held responsible for results.

VII. EMPLOYEE RELATIONSHIPS

   A. The employees reporting to one executive should not exceed the number which can be effectively directed and coordinated. The number will depend largely upon the scope and extent of the responsibilities of the subordinates.
   B. No person should report to more than one supervisor. Every supervisor should know who reports to him, and every employee should know to whom he reports. Channels of authority and responsibility should not be violated by staff units.
   C. Relationships between organizational units within the agency and with outside organizations and associations should be clearly stated and thoroughly understood to avoid misunderstanding.

DELEGATING

I. WHAT IS DELEGATING?
Delegating is assigning a job to an employee, giving him the authority to get that job done, and giving him the responsibility for seeing to it that the job is done.

   A. What To Delegate
      1. Routine details
      2. Jobs which may be necessary and take a lot of time, but do not have to be done by the supervisor personally (preparing reports, attending meetings, etc.)
      3. Routine decision-making (making decisions which do not require the supervisor's personal attention)

   B. What Not To Delegate
      1. Job details which are *executive functions* (setting goals, organizing employees into a good team, analyzing results so as to plan for the future)
      2. Disciplinary power (handling grievances, preparing service ratings, reprimands, etc.)
      3. Decision-making which involves large numbers of employees or other bureaus and departments
      4. Final and complete responsibility for the job done by the unit being supervised

   C. Why Delegate?
      1. To strengthen the organization by developing a greater number of skilled employees
      2. To improve the employee's performance by giving him the chance to learn more about the job, handle some responsibility, and become more interested in getting the job done
      3. To improve a supervisor's performance by relieving him of routine jobs and giving him more time for *executive functions* (planning, organizing, controlling, etc.) which cannot be delegated

II. TO WHOM TO DELEGATE
People with abilities not being used. Selection should be based on ability, not on favoritism.

REPORTS

I. **DEFINITION**
A report is an orderly presentation of factual information directed to a specific reader for a specific purpose

II. **PURPOSE**
The general purpose of a report is to bring to the reader useful and factual information about a condition or a problem. Some specific purposes of a report may be:

   A. To enable the reader to appraise the efficiency or effectiveness of a person or an operation
   B. To provide a basis for establishing standards
   C. To reflect the results of expenditures of time, effort, and money
   D. To provide a basis for developing or altering programs

III. **TYPES**

   A. Information Report: Contains facts arranged in sequence
   B. Summary (Examination) Report: Contains facts plus an analysis or discussion of the significance of the facts. Analysis may give advantages and disadvantages or give qualitative and quantitative comparisons
   C. Recommendation Report: Contains facts, analysis, and conclusion logically drawn from the facts and analysis, plus a recommendation based upon the facts, analysis, and conclusions

IV. **FACTORS TO CONSIDER BEFORE WRITING REPORT**

   A. <u>Why</u> write the report?: The purpose of the report should be clearly defined.
   B. <u>Who</u> will read the report?: What level of language should be used? Will the reader understand professional or technical language?
   C. <u>What</u> should be said?: What does the reader need or want to know about the subject?
   D. <u>How</u> should it be said?: Should the subject be presented tactfully? Convincingly? In a stimulating manner?

V. **PREPARATORY STEPS**

   A. Assemble the facts: Find out who, why, what, where, when, and how.
   B. Organize the facts: Eliminate unnecessary information
   C. Prepare an outline: Check for orderliness, logical sequence
   D. Prepare a draft: Check for correctness, clearness, completeness, conciseness, and tone
   E. Prepare it in final form: Check for grammar, punctuation, appearance

VI. **OUTLINE FOR A RECOMMENDATION REPORT**

   Is the report:
   A. Correct in information, grammar, and tone?
   B. Clear?
   C. Complete?

D. Concise?
E. Timely?
F. Worth its cost?

Will the report accomplish its purpose?

MANAGEMENT CONTROLS

I. CONTROL
What is control? What is controlled? Who controls?

The essence of control is action which adjusts operations to predetermined standards, and its basis is information in the hands of managers. Control is checking to determine whether plans are being observed and suitable progress toward stated objectives is being made, and action is taken, if necessary, to correct deviations.

We have a ready-made model for this concept of control in the automatic systems which are widely used for process control in the chemical land petroleum industries. A process control system works this way. Suppose, for example, it is desired to maintain a constant rate of flow of oil through a pipe at a predetermined or set-point value. A signal, whose strength represents the rate of flow, can be produced in a measuring device and transmitted to a control mechanism. The control mechanism, when it detects any deviation of the actual from the set-point signal, will reposition the value regulating flow rate.

II. BASIS FOR CONTROL

A process control mechanism thus acts to adjust operations to predetermined standards and does so on the basis of information it receives. In a parallel way, information reaching a manager gives him the opportunity for corrective action and is his basis for control. He cannot exercise control without such information, and he cannot do a complete job of managing without controlling.

III. POLICY

What is policy?

Policy is simply a statement of an organization's intention to act in certain ways when specified types of circumstances arise. It represents a general decision, predetermined and expressed as a principle or rule, establishing a normal pattern of conduct for dealing with given types of business events—usually recurrent. A statement is therefore useful in economizing the time of managers and in assisting them to discharge their responsibilities equitably and consistently.

Policy is not a means of control, but policy does generate the need for control.

Adherence to policies is not guaranteed nor can it be taken on faith. It has to be verified. Without verification, there is no basis for control. Policy and procedures, although closely related and interdependent to a certain extent, are not synonymous. A policy may be adopted, for example, to maintain a materials inventory not to exceed one million dollars.

A procedure for inventory control could interpret that policy and convert it into methods for keeping within that limit, with consideration, too, of possible but foreseeable expedient deviation.

IV. PROCEDURE

What is procedure?

A procedure specifically prescribes:
A. What work is to be performed by the various participants
B. Who are the respective participants
C. When and where the various steps in the different processes are to be performed
D. The sequence of operations that will insure uniform handling of recurring transactions
E. The paper that is involved, its origin, transition, and disposition

Necessary appurtenances to a procedure are:
A. Detailed organizational chart
B. Flow charts
C. Exhibits of forms, all presented in close proximity to the text of the procedure

V. BASIS OF CONTROL – INFORMATION IN THE HANDS OF MANAGERS

If the basis of control is information in the hands of managers, then reporting is elevated to a level of very considerable importance.

Types of reporting may include:
A. Special reports and routine reports
B. Written, oral, and graphic reports
C. Staff meetings
D. Conferences
E. Television screens
F. Non-receipt of information, as where management is by exception
G. Any other means whereby information is transmitted to a manager as a basis for control action

FRAMEWORK OF MANAGEMENT

I. ELEMENTS

   A. Policy: It has to be verified, controlled.

   B. Organization is part of the giving of an assignment. The organizational chart gives to each individual in his title, a first approximation of the nature of his assignment and orients him as being accountable to a certain individual. Organization is not in a true sense a means of control. Control is checking to ascertain whether the assignment is executed as intended and acting on the basis of that information.

   C. Budgets perform three functions:
      1. They present the objectives, plans, and programs of the organization in financial terms.

2. They report the progress of actual performance against these predetermined objectives, plans, and programs.
3. Like organizational charts, delegations of authority, procedures, and job descriptions, they define the assignments which have flowed from the Chief Executive. Budgets are a means of control in the respect that they report progress of actual performance against the program. They provide information which enables managers to take action directed toward bringing actual results into conformity with the program.

D. Internal Check provides in practice for the principle that the same person should not have responsibility for all phases of a transaction. This makes it clearly an aspect of organization rather than of control. Internal Check is static, or built-in.

E. Plans, Programs, Objectives
People must know what they are trying to do. Objectives fulfill this need. Without them, people may work industriously and yet, working aimlessly, accomplish little. Plans and Programs complement Objectives, since they propose how and according to what time schedule the objectives are to be reached.

F. Delegations of Authority
Among the ways we have for supplementing the titles and lines of authority of an organizational chart are delegations of authority. Delegations of authority clarify the extent of authority of individuals and in that way serve to define assignments. That they are not means of control is apparent from the very fact that wherever there has been a delegation of authority, the need for control increases. This could hardly be expected to happen if delegations of authority were themselves means of control.

II. MANAGER'S RESPONSIBILITY

Control becomes necessary whenever a manager delegates authority to a subordinate because he cannot delegate and then simply sit back and forget4 about it. A manager's accountability to his own superior has not diminished one whit as a result of delegating part of his authority to a subordinate. The manager must exercise control over actions taken under the authority so delegated. That means checking serves as a basis for possible corrective action.

Objectives, plans, programs, organizational charts, and other elements of the managerial system are not fruitfully regarded as either controls or means of control. They are pre-established standards or models of performance to which operations are adjusted by the exercise of management control. These standards or models of performance are dynamic in character for they are constantly altered, modified, or revised. Policies, organizational set-up, procedures, delegations, etc. are constantly altered but, like objectives and plans, they remain in force until they are either abandoned or revised. All of the elements (or standards or models of performance), objectives, plans, and programs, policies, organization, etc. can be regarded as a *framework of management*.

III. CONTROL TECHNIQUES

Examples of control techniques:
A. Compare against established standards
B. Compare with a similar operation
C. Compare with past operations
D. Compare with predictions of accomplishment

IV. WHERE FORECASTS FIT

Control is after-the-fact while forecasts are before. Forecasts and projections are important for setting objectives and formulating plans.

Information for aiming and planning does not have to be before-the-fact. It may be an after-the-fact analysis proving that a certain policy has been impolitic in its effect on the relation of the company or department with customer, employee, taxpayer, or stockholder; or that a certain plan is no longer practical, or that a certain procedure is unworkable.

The prescription here certainly would not be in control (in these cases, control would simply bring operations into conformity with obsolete standards) but the establishment of new standards, a new policy, a new plan, and a new procedure to be controlled too.

Information is, of course, the basis for all communication in addition to furnishing evidence to management of the need for reconstructing the framework of management.

PROBLEM SOLVING

The accepted concept in modern management for problem solving is the utilization of the following steps:

A. Identify the problem
B. Gather data
C. List possible solutions
D. Test possible solutions
E. Select the best solution
F. Put the solution into actual practice

Occasions might arise where you would have to apply the second step of gathering data before completing the first step.

You might also find that it will be necessary to work on several steps at the same time.

I. IDENTIFY THE PROBLEM

Your first step is to define as precisely as possible the problem to be solved. While this may sound easy, it is often the most difficult part of the process.

It has been said of problem solving that you are halfway to the solution when you can write out a clear statement of the problem itself.

Our job now is to get below the surface manifestations of the trouble and pinpoint the problem. This is usually accomplished by a logical analysis, by going from the general to the particular; from the obvious to the not-so-obvious cause.

Let us say that production is behind schedule. WHY? Absenteeism is high. Now, is absenteeism the basic problem to be tackled, or is it merely a symptom of low morale among the workforce? Under these circumstances, you may decide that production is not the problem; the problem is *employee morale*.

In trying to define the problem, remember there is seldom one simple reason why production is lagging, or reports are late, etc.

Analysis usually leads to the discovery that an apparent problem is really made up of several subproblems which must be attacked separately.

Another way is to limit the problem, and thereby ease the task of finding a solution, and concentrate on the elements which are within the scope of your control.

When you have gone this far, write out a tentative statement of the problem to be solved.

II. GATHER DATA

In the second step, you must set out to collect all the information that might have a bearing on the problem. Do not settle for an assumption when reasonable fact and figures are available.

If you merely go through the motions of problem-solving, you will probably shortcut the information-gathering step. Therefore, do not stack the evidence by confining your research to your own preconceived ideas.

As you collect facts, organize them in some form that helps you make sense of them and spot possible relationships between them. For example, plotting cost per unit figures on a graph can be more meaningful than a long column of figures.

Evaluate each item as you go along. Is the source material absolutely, reliable, probably reliable, or not to be trusted.

One of the best methods for gathering data is to go out and look the situation over carefully. Talk to the people on the job who are most affected by this problem.

Always keep in mind that a primary source is usually better than a secondary source of information.

III. LIST POSSIBLE SOLUTIONS

This is the creative thinking step of problem solving. This is a good time to bring into play whatever techniques of group dynamics the agency or bureau might have developed for a joint attack on problems.

Now the important thing for you to do is: Keep an open mind. Let your imagination roam freely over the facts you have collected. Jot down every possible solution that occurs to you. Resist the temptation to evaluate various proposals as you go along. List seemingly absurd ideas along with more plausible ones. The more possibilities you list during this step, the less risk you will run of settling for merely a workable, rather than the best, solution.

Keep studying the data as long as there seems to be any chance of deriving additional ideas, solutions, explanations, or patterns from it.

IV. TEST POSSIBLE SOLUTIONS

Now you begin to evaluate the possible solutions. Take pains to be objective. Up to this point, you have suspended judgment but you might be tempted to select a solution you secretly favored all along and proclaim it as the best of the lot.

The secret of objectivity in this phase is to test the possible solutions separately, measuring each against a common yardstick. To make this yardstick try to enumerate as many specific criteria as you can think of. Criteria are best phrased as questions which you ask of each possible solution. They can be drawn from these general categories:

Suitability – Will this solution do the job?
Will it solve the problem completely or partially?
Is it a permanent or a stopgap solution?

Feasibility - Will this plan work in actual practice?
Can we afford this approach?
How much will it cost?

Acceptability - Will the boss go along with the changes required in the plan?
Are we trying to drive a tack with a sledge hammer?

V. SELECT THE BEST SOLUTION

This is the area of executive decision.

Occasionally, one clearly superior solution will stand out at the conclusion of the testing process. But often it is not that simple. You may find that no one solution has come through all the tests with flying colors.

You may also find that a proposal, which flunked miserably on one of the essential tests, racked up a very high score on others.

The best solution frequently will turn out to be a combination.

Try to arrange a marriage that will bring together the strong points of one possible solution with the particular virtues of another. The more skill and imagination that you apply, the greater is the likelihood that you will come out with a solution that is not merely adequate and workable, but is the best possible under the circumstances.

VI. PUT THE SOLUTION INTO ACTUAL PRACTICE

As every executive knows, a plan which works perfectly on paper may develop all sorts of bugs when put into actual practice.

Problem-solving does not stop with selecting the solution which looks best in theory. The next step is to put the chosen solution into action and watch the results. The results may point towards modifications.

If the problem disappears when you put your solution into effect, you know you have the right solution.

If it does not disappear, even after you have adjusted your plan to cover unforeseen difficulties that turned up in practice, work your way back through the problem-solving solutions.

> Would one of them have worked better?
> Did you overlook some vital piece of data which would have given you a different slant on the whole situation? Did you apply all necessary criteria in testing solutions? If no light dawns after this much rechecking, it is a pretty good bet that you defined the problem incorrectly in the first place.

You came up with the wrong solution because you tackled the wrong problem.

Thus, step six may become step one of a new problem-solving cycle.

COMMUNICATION

I. WHAT IS COMMUNICATION?
We communicate through writing, speaking, action, or inaction. In speaking to people face-to-face, there is opportunity to judge reactions and to adjust the message. This makes the supervisory chain one of the most, and in many instances the most, important channels of communication.

In an organization, communication means keeping employees informed about the organization's objectives, policies, problems, and progress. Communication is the free interchange of information, ideas, and desirable attitudes between and among employees and between employees and management.

II. WHY IS COMMUNICATION NEEDED?

  A. People have certain social needs
  B. Good communication is essential in meeting those social needs
  C. While people have similar basic needs, at the same time they differ from each other
  D. Communication must be adapted to these individual differences

An employee cannot do his best work unless he knows why he is doing it. If he has the feeling that he is being kept in the dark about what is going on, his enthusiasm and productivity suffer.

Effective communication is needed in an organization so that employees will understand what the organization is trying to accomplish; and how the work of one unit contributes to or affects the work of other units in the organization and other organizations.

III. HOW IS COMMUNICATION ACHIEVED?

Communication flows downward, upward, sideways.

A. Communication may come from top management down to employees. This is downward communication.

   Some means of downward communication are:
   1. Training (orientation, job instruction, supervision, public relations, etc.)
   2. Conferences
   3. Staff meetings
   4. Policy statements
   5. Bulletins
   6. Newsletters
   7. Memoranda
   8. Circulation of important letters

   In downward communication, it is important that employees be informed in advance of changes that will affect them.

B. Communications should also be developed so that the ideas, suggestions, and knowledge of employees will flow upward to top management.

   Some means of upward communication are:
   1. Personal discussion conferences
   2. Committees
   3. Memoranda
   4. Employees suggestion program
   5. Questionnaires to be filled in giving comments and suggestions about proposed actions that will affect field operations.

   Upward communication requires that management be willing to listen, to accept, and to make changes when good ideas are present. Upward communication succeeds when there is no fear of punishment for speaking out or lack of interest at the top. Employees will share their knowledge and ideas with management when interest is shown and recognition is given.

C. The advantages of downward communication:
   1. It enables the passing down of orders, policies, and plans necessary to the continued operation of the station.
   2. By making information available, it diminishes the fears and suspicions which result from misinformation and misunderstanding.
   3. It fosters the pride people want to have in their work when they are told of good work.
   4. It improves the morale and stature of the individual to be *in the know*.

5. It helps employees to understand, accept, and cooperate with changes when they know about them in advance.

D. The advantages of upward communication:
1. It enables the passing upward of information, attitudes, and feelings.
2. It makes it easier to find out how ready people are to receive downward communication.
3. It reveals the degree to which the downward communication is understood and accepted.
4. It helps to satisfy the basic social needs.
5. It stimulates employees to participate in the operation of their organization.
6. It encourage employees to contribute ideas for improving the efficiency and economy of operations.
7. It helps to solve problem situations before they reach the explosion point.

IV. WHY DOES COMMUNICATION FAIL?

A. The technical difficulties of conveying information clearly
B. The emotional content of communication which prevents complete transmission
C. The fact that there is a difference between what management needs to say, what it wants to day, and what it does say
D. The fact that there is a difference between what employees would like to say, what they think is profitable or safe to say, and what they do say

V. HOW TO IMPROVE COMMUNICATION

As a supervisor, you are a key figure in communication. To improve as a communicator, you should:
A. Know: Knowing your subordinates will help you to recognize and work with individual differences.
B. Like: If you like those who work for you and those for whom you work, this will foster the kind of friendly, warm, work atmosphere that will facilitate communication.
C. Trust: Showing a sincere desire to communicate will help to develop the mutual trust and confidence which are essential to the free flow of communication.
D. Tell: Tell your subordinates and superiors *what's doing*. Tell your subordinates *why* as well as *how*.
E. Listen: By listening, you help others to talk and you create good listeners. Don't forget that listening implies action.
F. Stimulate: Communication has to be stimulated and encouraged. Be receptive to ideas and suggestions and motivate your people so that each member of the team identifies himself with the job at hand.
G. Consult: The most effective way of consulting is to let your people participate, insofar as possible, in developing determinations which affect them or their work.

VI. HOW TO DETERMINE WHETHER YOU ARE GETTING ACROSS

A. Check to see that communication is received and understood
B. Judge this understanding by actions rather than words
C. Adapt or vary communication, when necessary
D. Remember that good communication cannot cure all problems

VII. THE KEY ATTITUDE

Try to see things from the other person's point of view. By doing this, you help to develop the permissive atmosphere and the shared confidence and understanding which are essential to effective two-way communication.

Communication is a two-way process:
A. The basic purpose of any communication is to get action.
B. The only way to get action is through acceptance.
C. In order to get acceptance, communication must be humanly satisfying as well as technically efficient.

HOW ORDERS AND INSTRUCTIONS SHOULD BE GIVEN

I. CHARACTERISTICS OF GOOD ORDERS AND INSTRUCTIONS

   A. Clear
      Orders should be definite as to
      —What is to be done
      —Who is to do it
      —When it is to be done
      —Where it is to be done
      —How it is to be done

   B. Concise
      Avoid wordiness. Orders should be brief and to the point.

   C. Timely
      Instructions and orders should be sent out at the proper time and not too long in advance of expected performance.

   D. Possibility of Performance
      Orders should be feasible:
      1. Investigate before giving orders
      2. Consult those who are to carry out instructions before formulating and issuing them

   E. Properly Directed
      Give the orders to the people concerned. Do not send orders to people who are not concerned. People who continually receive instructions that are not applicable to them get in the habit of neglecting instructions generally.

   F. Reviewed Before Issuance
      Orders should be reviewed before issuance:
      1. Test them by putting yourself in the position of the recipient
      2. If they involve new procedures, have the persons who are to do the work review them for suggestions.

   G. Reviewed After Issuance
      Persons who receive orders should be allowed to raise questions and to point out unforeseen consequences of orders.

H. Coordinated
Orders should be coordinated so that work runs smoothly.

I. Courteous
Make a request rather than a demand. There is no need to continually call attention to the fact that you are the boss.

J. Recognizable as an Order
Be sure that the order is recognizable as such.

K. Complete
Be sure recipient has knowledge and experience sufficient to carry out order. Give illustrations and examples.

A DEPARTMENTAL PERSONNEL OFFICE IS RESPONSIBLE FOR THE FOLLOWING FUNCTIONS

1. Policy
2. Personnel Programs
3. Recruitment and Placement
4. Position Classification
5. Salary and Wage Administration
6. Employee performance Standards and Evaluation
7. Employee Relations
8. Disciplinary Actions and Separations
9. Health and Safety
10. Staff Training and Development
11. Personnel Records, Procedures, and Reports
12. Employee Services
13. Personnel Research

SUPERVISION

I. LEADERSHIP

All leadership is based essentially on authority. This comes from two sources: It is received from higher management or it is earned by the supervisor through his methods of supervision. Although effective leadership has always depended upon the leader's using his authority in such a way as to appeal successfully to the motives of the people supervised, the conditions for making this appeal are continually changing. The key to today's problem of leadership is flexibility and resourcefulness on the part of the leader in meeting changes in conditions as they occur.

Three basic approaches to leadership are generally recognized:

A. The Authoritarian Approach
   1. The methods and techniques used in this approach emphasize the *I* in leadership and depend primarily on the formal authority of the leader. This authority is sometimes exercised in a hardboiled manner and sometimes in a benevolent

manner, but in either case the dominating role of the leader is reflected in the thinking, planning, and decisions of the group.
2. Group results are to a large degree dependent on close supervision by the leader. Usually, the individuals in the group will not show a high degree of initiative or acceptance of responsibility and their capacity to grow and develop probably will not be fully utilized. The group may react with resentment or submission, depending upon the manner and skill of the leader in using his authority.
3. This approach develops as a natural outgrowth of the authority that goes with the leader's job and his feeling of sole responsibility for getting the job done. It is relatively easy to use and does not require must resourcefulness.
4. The use of this approach is effective in times of emergencies, in meeting close deadline as a final resort, in settling some issues, in disciplinary matters, and with dependent individuals and groups.

B. The Laissez-Faire or Let 'em Alone Approach
1. This approach generally is characterized by an avoidance of leadership responsibility by the leader. The activities of the group depend largely on the choice of its members rather than the leader.
2. Group results probably will be poor. Generally, there will be disagreements over petty things, bickering, and confusion. Except for a few aggressive people, individuals will not show much initiative and growth and development will be retarded. There may be a tendency for informal leaders to take over leadership of the group.
3. This approach frequently results from the leader's dislike of responsibility, from his lack of confidence, from failure of other methods to work, from disappointment or criticism. It is usually the easiest of the three to use and requires both understanding and resourcefulness on the part of the leader.
4. This approach is occasionally useful and effective, particularly in forcing dependent individuals or groups to rely on themselves, to give someone a chance to save face by clearing his own difficulties, or when action should be delayed temporarily for good cause.

C. The Democratic Approach
1. The methods and techniques used in this approach emphasize the *we* in leadership and build up the responsibility of the group to attain its objectives. Reliance is placed largely on the earned authority of the leader.
2. Group results are likely to be good because most of the job motives of the people will be satisfied. Cooperation and teamwork, initiative, acceptance of responsibility, and the individual's capacity for growth probably will show a high degree of development.
3. This approach grows out of a desire or necessity of the leader to find ways to appeal effectively to the motivation of his group. It is the best approach to build up inside the person a strong desire to cooperate and apply himself to the job. It is the most difficult to develop, and requires both understanding and resourcefulness on the part of the leader.
4. The value of this approach increases over a long period where sustained efficiency and development of people are important. It may not be fully effective in all situations, however, particularly when there is not sufficient time to use it properly or where quick decisions must be made.

All three approaches are used by most leaders and have a place in supervising people. The extent of their use varies with individual leaders, with some using one approach predominantly. The leader who uses these three approaches, and varies their use with time and circumstance, is probably the most effective. Leadership which is used predominantly with a democratic approach requires more resourcefulness on the part of the leader but offers the greatest possibilities in terms of teamwork and cooperation.

The one best way of developing democratic leadership is to provide a real sense of participation on the part of the group, since this satisfies most of the chief job motives. Although there are many ways of providing participation, consulting as frequently as possible with individuals and groups on things that affect them seems to offer the most in building cooperation and responsibility. Consultation takes different forms, but it is most constructive when people feel they are actually helping in finding the answers to the problems on the job.

There are some requirements of leaders in respect to human relations which should be considered in their selection and development. Generally, the leader should be interested in working with other people, emotionally stable, self-confident, and sensitive to the reactions of others. In addition, his viewpoint should be one of getting the job done through people who work cooperatively in response to his leadership. He should have a knowledge of individual and group behavior, but, most important of all, he should work to combine all of these requirements into a definite, practical skill in leadership.

II. NINE POINTS OF CONTRAST BETWEEN *BOSS* AND *LEADER*

   A. The boss drives his men; the leader coaches them.
   B. The boss depends on authority; the leader on good will.
   C. The boss inspires fear; the leader inspires enthusiasm.
   D. The boss says I; the leader says *We*.
   E. The boss says *Get here on time*; the leader gets there ahead of time.
   F. The boss fixes the blame for the breakdown; the leader fixes the breakdown.
   G. The boss knows how it is done; the leader shows how.
   H. The boss makes work a drudgery; the leader makes work a game.
   I. The boss says *Go*; the leader says *Let's go*.

EMPLOYEE MORALE

Employee morale is the way employees feel about each other, the organization or unit in which they work, and the work they perform.

I. SOME WAYS TO DEVELOP AND MAINTAIN GOOD EMPLYEE MORALE

   A. Give adequate credit and praise when due.
   B. Recognize importance of all jobs and equalize load with proper assignments, always giving consideration to personality differences and abilities.
   C. Welcome suggestions and do not have an *all-wise* attitude. Request employees' assistance in solving problems and use assistants when conducting group meetings on certain subjects.
   D. Properly assign responsibilities and give adequate authority for fulfillment of such assignments.

E. Keep employees informed about matters that affect them.
F. Criticize and reprimand employees privately.
G. Be accessible and willing to listen.
H. Be fair.
I. Be alert to detect training possibilities so that you will not miss an opportunity to help each employee do a better job, and if possible with less effort on his part.
J. Set a good example.
K. Apply the golden rule.

II. SOME INDICATIONS OF GOOD MORALE

A. Good quality of work
B. Good quantity
C. Good attitude of employees
D. Good discipline
E. Teamwork
F. Good attendance
G. Employee participation

MOTIVATION

DRIVES

A drive, stated simply, is a desire or force which causes a person to do or say certain things. These are some of the most usual drives and some of their identifying characteristics recognizable in people motivated by such drives:

A. Security (desire to provide for the future)
   Always on time for work
   Works for the same employer for many years
   Never takes unnecessary chances
   Seldom resists doing what he is told

B. Recognition (desire to be rewarded for accomplishment)
   Likes to be asked for his opinion
   Becomes very disturbed when he makes a mistake
   Does things to attract attention
   Likes to see his name in print

C. Position (desire to hold certain status in relation to others)
   Boasts about important people he knows
   Wants to be known as a key man
   Likes titles
   Demands respect
   Belongs to clubs, for prestige

D. Accomplishment (desire to get things done)
   Complains when things are held up
   Likes to do things that have tangible results
   Never lies down on the job
   Is proud of turning out good work

E. Companionship (desire to associate with other people)
   Likes to work with others
   Tells stories and jokes
   Indulges in horseplay
   Finds excuses to talk to others on the job

F. Possession (desire to collect and hoard objects)
   Likes to collect things
   Puts his name on things belonging to him
   Insists on the same location

Supervisors may find that identifying the drives of employees is a helpful step toward motivating them to self-improvement and better job performance. For example: An employee's job performance is below average. His supervisor, having previously determined that the employee is motivated by a drive for security, suggests that taking training courses will help the employee to improve, advance, and earn more money. Since earning more money can be a step toward greater security, the employee's drive for security would motivate him to take the training suggested by the supervisor. In essence, this is the process of charting an employee's future course by using his motivating drives to positive advantage.

EMPLOYEE PARTICIPATION

I. WHAT IS PARTICIPATION

Employee participation is the employee's giving freely of his time, skill, and knowledge to an extent which cannot be obtained by demand.

II. WHY IS IT IMPORTANT?

The supervisor's responsibility is to get the job done through people. A good supervisor gets the job done through people who work willingly and well. The participation of employees is important because:

A. Employees develop a greater sense of responsibility when they share in working out operating plans and goals.
B. Participation provides greater opportunity and stimulation for employees to learn, and to develop their ability.
C. Participation sometimes provides better solutions to problems because such solutions may combine the experience and knowledge of interested employees who want the solutions to work.
D. An employee or group may offer a solution which the supervisor might hesitate to make for fear of demanding too much.

E. Since the group wants to make the solution work, they exert pressure in a constructive way on each other.
F. Participation usually results in reducing the need for close supervision.

II. HOW MAY SUPERVISORS OBTAIN IT?

Participation is encouraged when employees feel that they share some responsibility for the work and that their ideas are sincerely wanted and valued. Some ways of obtaining employee participation are:

A. Conduct orientation programs for new employees to inform them about the organization and their rights and responsibilities as employees.
B. Explain the aims and objectives of the agency. On a continuing basis, be sure that the employees know what these aims and objectives are.
C. Share job successes and responsibilities and give credit for success.
D. Consult with employees, both as individuals and in groups, about things that affect them.
E. Encourage suggestions for job improvements. Help employees to develop good suggestions. The suggestions can bring them recognition. The city's suggestion program offers additional encouragement through cash awards.

The supervisor who encourages employee participation is not surrendering his authority. He must still make decisions and initiate action, and he must continue to be ultimately responsible for the work of those he supervises. But, through employee participation, he is helping his group to develop greater ability and a sense of responsibility while getting the job done faster and better.

STEPS IN HANDLING A GRIEVANCE

1. Get the Facts
   a. Listen sympathetically
   b. Let him talk himself out
   c. Get his story straight
   d. Get his point of view
   e. Don't argue with him
   f. Give him plenty of time
   g. Conduct the interview privately
   h. Don't try to shift the blame or pass the buck

2. Consider the Facts
   a. Consider the employee's viewpoint
   b. How will the decision affect similar cases
   c. Consider each decision as a possible precedent
   d. Avoid snap judgments—don't jump to conclusions

3. Make or Get a Decision
   a. Frame an effective counter-proposal
   b. Make sure it is fair to all
   c. Have confidence in your judgment
   d. Be sure you can substantiate your decision

4. Notify the Employee of Your Decision
   Be sure he is told; try to convince him that the decision is fair and just.

5. Take Action When Needed and If Within Your Authority
   Otherwise, tell employee that the matter will be called to the attention of the proper person or that nothing can be done, and why it cannot.

6. Follow through to see that the desired result is achieved.

7. Record key facts concerning the complaint and the action taken.

8. Leave the way open to him to appeal your decision to a higher authority.

9. Report all grievances to your superior, whether they are appealed or not.

DISCIPLINE

Discipline is training that develops self-control, orderly conduct, and efficiency.

To discipline does not necessarily mean to punish.

To discipline does mean to train, to regulate, and to govern conduct.

I. THE DISCIPLINARY INTERVIEW

Most employees sincerely want to do what is expected of them. In other words, they are self-disciplined. Some employees, however, fail to observe established rules and standards, and disciplinary action by the supervisor is required.

The primary purpose of disciplinary action is to improve conduct without creating dissatisfaction, bitterness, or resentment in the process.

Constructive disciplinary action is more concerned with causes and explanations of breaches of conduct than with punishment. The disciplinary interview is held to get at the causes of apparent misbehavior and to motivate better performance in the future.

It is important that the interview be kept on an impersonal a basis as possible. If the supervisor lets the interview descend to the plane of an argument, it loses its effectiveness.

II. PLANNING THE INTERVIEW

Get all pertinent facts concerning the situation so that you can talk in specific terms to the employee.

Review the employee's record, appraisal ratings, etc.

Consider what you know about the temperament of the employee. Consider your attitude toward the employee. Remember that the primary requisite of disciplinary action is fairness.

Don't enter upon the interview when angry.

Schedule the interview for a place which is private and out of hearing of others.

III. CONDUCTING THE INTERVIEW

A. Make an effort to establish accord.
B. Question the employee about the apparent breach of discipline. Be sure that the question is not so worded as to be itself an accusation.
C. Give the employee a chance to tell his side of the story. Give him ample opportunity to talk.
D. Use understanding—listening except where it is necessary to ask a question or to point out some details of which the employee may not be aware. If the employee misrepresents facts, make a plain, accurate statement of the facts, but don't argue and don't engage in personal controversy.
E. Listen and try to understand the reasons for the employee's (mis)conduct. First of all, don't assume that there has been a breach of discipline. Evaluate the employee's reasons for his conduct in the light of his opinions and feelings concerning the consistency and reasonableness of the standards which he was expected to follow. Has the supervisor done his part in explaining the reasons for the rule? Was the employee's behavior unintentional or deliberate? Does he think he had real reasons for his actions? What new facts is he telling? Do the facts justify his actions? What causes, other than those mentioned, could have stimulated the behavior?
F. After listening to the employee's version of the situation, and if censure of his actions is warranted, the supervisor should proceed with whatever criticism is justified. Emphasis should be placed on future improvement rather than exclusively on the employee's failure to measure up to expected standards of job conduct.
G. Fit the criticism to the individual. With one employee, a word of correction may be all that is required.
H. Attempt to distinguish between unintentional error and deliberate misbehavior. An error due to ignorance requires training and not censure.
I. Administer criticism in a controlled, even tone of voice, never in anger. Make it clear that you are acting as an agent of the department. In general, criticism should refer to the job or the employee's actions and not to the person. Criticism of the employee's work is not an attack on the individual.
J. Be sure the interview does not destroy the employee's self-confidence. Mention his good qualities and assure him that you feel confident that he can improve his performance.
K. Wherever possible, before the employee leaves the interview, satisfy him that the incident is closed, that nothing more will be said on the subject unless the offense is repeated.

www.ingramcontent.com/pod-product-compliance
Lightning Source LLC
Chambersburg PA
CBHW081822300426
44116CB00014B/2452